Sync Your Soul

God's Still With You

Sue Marie Gerard

Sync Your Soul | Sue Gerard

Copyright © 2018 All rights Reserved.

All rights reserved. No part of this publication may be reproduced, distributed, or transmitted in any form or by any means, including photocopying, recording, or other electronic or mechanical methods, without the prior written permission of the publisher, except in the case of brief quotations embodied in critical reviews and certain other noncommercial uses permitted by copyright law.

Scriptures taken from the Holy Bible, New International Version®, NIV®. Copyright © 1973, 1978, 1984, 2011 by Biblica, Inc.™ Used by permission of Zondervan. All rights reserved worldwide. www.zondervan.com The "NIV" and "New International Version" are trademarks registered in the United States Patent and Trademark Office by Biblica, Inc.™

When life's twists and turns leave you feeling lost, confused, and out of balance, sync your heart, thoughts and Faith with God as your center to become whole once again.

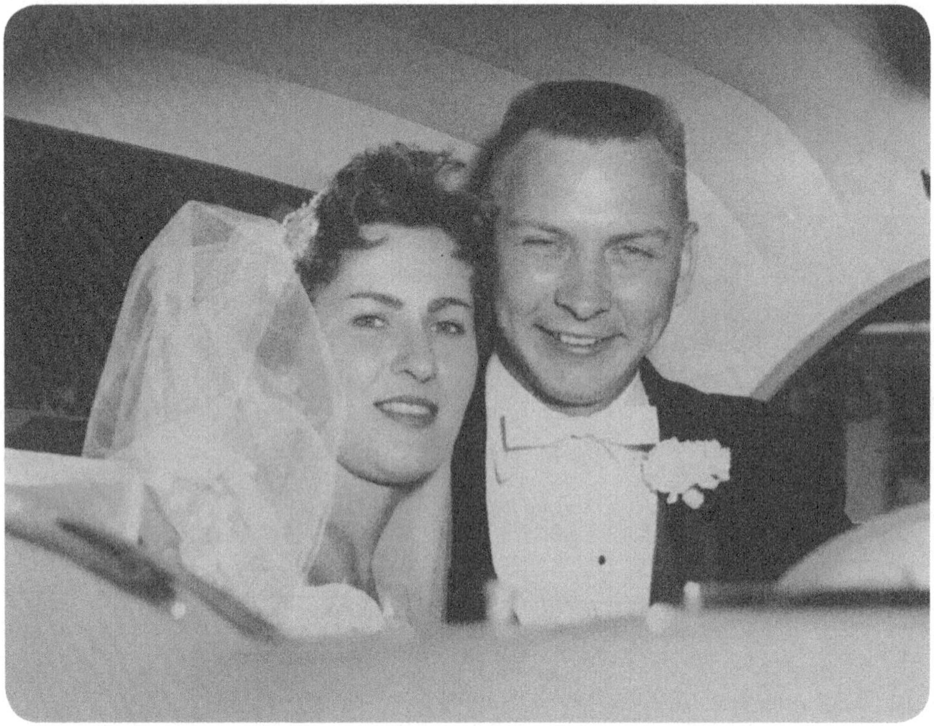

Dedication

This book is dedicated to my Mom and Dad, who left their legacies of faith, perseverance, and the true meaning of family. Though they are no longer here on this earth, their spirits live on within my heart, as their life examples continue to fill me with wisdom, direction, and love.

Acknowledgements

First, I would like to thank God for inspiring my heart and trusting me to go on this wonderful journey with Him. This book truly represents that "all things are possible with Him."

I am also so grateful to my family and friends who encouraged and supported me in every step that I took.

My Hubby Tom, who always lifted me up when I wanted to give up. My daughter Sarah who was always willing to read every message I sent to her and offer her loving advice and support. My dear friend and soul sister Char, who knows my heart better than I do myself and always brought balance when I felt like I was falling over. My son-in-law George who graciously gave me some of the amazing photos here, and my Dearest Katie who helped in ways that only she could.

To all my dear friends at the Little Somethin' Something FB Page who lift me up every day and inspire me to continue writing, as well as to Melinda Martin, my publisher, who was always patient, kind and could see my visions better than I could.

And lastly to my dear Dr. Carlton Lyons, who many years ago told me to write and planted the seed that began this beautiful journey.

I am humbly blessed in every way and grateful beyond measure for all the love and support God brought to me to be able to write this book and share it with all of you.

Introduction

Hello! I'm Sue and it's so very nice to meet you! I'm so excited that you are here to share in the journey of my very first book.

The inspirations I share come from the deep and personal places within my heart; life encounters that I have walked through in my own life. The heartaches, the lessons, the storms, the wisdom, and the amazing blessings that God has bestowed upon me which have shaped me into who I am today. I share this brief synopsis of my life with you, so you may see God's amazing hand in my life, and to connect on a deeper level with each inspiration, as it speaks to your heart and brings its own personal message to you in the way God intends it to.

My true spiritual journey began in my early twenties, so I will begin there.

I married young at twenty-two, and seven years later I found myself divorced! I honestly never saw that coming, in any way, shape or form. We were trying to get pregnant when I found out he was having an affair, and on a turn of a dime my life changed forever. I asked God "Why?" What did I do to deserve this, and why did you let this happen to me? It was these very questions that initiated the greatest and most important step in my own faith journey to dig deeper into a true "relationship" with Him.

My Dad had a true heart for God, always seeking and searching for more. He inspired me to move beyond the teachings of the "religion" I grew up in, a religion that brought a great amount of guilt and condemnation to my heart. Though my faith was young and confused, I came to realize that this was the best place to be in my life, for it brought many questions, which lead me to the answers I was searching for. God carried me through this season of my life with His grace, mercy, favor, and protection, even though in these moments I had yet to discover the God who so loved me unconditionally.

After going through the storm of divorce, I met my husband Tom, and we were married a few years later. We had our beautiful daughter Sarah, who became the love and joy of our lives, completing our family of three (for now), which ended up being our family of three forever.

I got pregnant again about 4 years after we had Sarah and sadly lost that baby to an early miscarriage. Two years later we were expecting again, only to lose this child as well. I was completely devastated and fell into a place of darkness, fear, anger, and confusion; a place I had never visited before and was definitely not prepared for.

Grieving a miscarriage is quite different than any other loss, for this child only existed within your womb, and left before having the chance to come out and meet us at the time of their birth. They are here one day and then suddenly gone the next, leaving a void that is unexplainable, especially to the mother who carried them. There is no funeral, no life celebration, no way to say a formal goodbye to this child you loved so deeply, and now you are lost in a place of grief that seems to have no possibility for healing or closure.

For the next two years I suffered tremendous anxiety, deep depression, and frequent panic attacks that would come out of nowhere. I feared death, I feared life, I feared being alone and being with others as well. I lived in a place so dark, a place I tried to hide deep within myself behind a mask, so that no one else would see me falling apart.

Life continued its downward spiral for the next few years, with many job losses leading to financial distress, bringing damage to our lives, family, and our marriage. Tom and I grew further and further apart as he shut down, and I became increasingly lonely, angry, overwhelmed, and lost.

These were the years I thought God had taken EVERYTHING away from me, and that He no longer loved me and just didn't care!

It didn't stop there unfortunately. My Dad, who was my rock here on earth, passed away in June of 2009, after a long seven years of continual problems that took him away slowly, piece by piece. Tom and I separated about a year or so later after my Dad's passing, thinking a break in all the chaos would somehow be the answer to "fix" us, and it definitely ended up being one of our biggest mistakes and didn't solve anything. One year evolved into two and a half long years of separation and almost a divorce, but thanks be to God, who had a different plan for us, our marriage was saved.

While we were still separated, my Mom had a major stroke, and though it was a true miracle that she lived, it changed our family structure and caused great hurt and discord among myself and my siblings.

My husband was gone, my family was broken, I felt so unloved, alone, rejected and abandoned. I became someone I didn't even know anymore, living in a place of utter hopelessness, a place so full of darkness, where I began to believe that the world would be better off without me.

I kept going for the sake of my daughter, knowing I could never leave or abandon her, yet feeling so very guilty that she had to endure all of this through no fault of her own, and that I had truly failed at being the Mom she deserved. But my daughter is strong and amazing, and she became my rock in many ways; even though that should have never been her role to play, she did it well through the grace and strength that God gave her to be that person for me.

Life seemed like a punching bag, as one strike continued after another, each punch landing harder and harder and beating me down even farther. Yet, it was in this very place of overwhelming devastation and hopelessness that I finally realized that God was waiting for me to reach out and lay all these burdens on His shoulders. Only then did I come to realize, the amazing God who loved me unconditionally, no matter what shape my life was in, even when I didn't see or believe. He was the one carrying me through everything with his love, grace, mercy, and never-ending compassion and protection. He never left or abandoned me, even when I was lost and walked away from Him.

God not only got me through these years of pain, challenge and all the trials I faced, He took something good from every experience, changed my heart, made me stronger, opened new doors for me to enter, and became the true light in my life.

My husband and I are now reunited and greatly blessed in our new journey together with God as our center, forming a stronger bond and connection with each other, while moving forward in ways I never before thought were possible. Sarah is married to a wonderful man and beginning the next chapter of her life. Our financial situation has greatly improved in amazing ways, and most of my family relationships are being healed. My faith has grown and my personal relationship with God is closer than I could ever have imagined or hoped for, and God has placed wonderful people in our lives to travel this journey together. He continues to bring new opportunities to fulfill each plan He calls us to, while bringing peace, blessings, and joy to our lives and those of others, according to His will and purpose for each of us.

It all began with the choice I made when I was at my lowest low, to reach for His hand in faith and trust, and invite him into my life completely. Embracing every weakness, vulnerable place, and fear within, handing it all over to Him, knowing that only He could restore all of these things and bring something good from this "life mess" that I found myself in…as He always does and always will, when we let go and let Him in.

    Always remember that God's "light" shines the brightest in the darkest of places; open your eyes, heart, and mind to find His light that is always there for you.

Live lovingly, blessed friends.

Sue Marie Gerard

> "You will seek and find me when you seek me with all of your heart."
> Jeremiah 29:13 NIV

> "Come to me, all you who are weary and burdened, and I will give you rest."
> Matthew 11:28 NIV

take it slow

"Therefore, as God's chosen people, holy and dearly loved,
clothe yourselves with compassion, kindness, humility, gentleness and patience."

Colossians 3:12 NIV

Pursue Your Patience

I read a book a couple of years ago about finding just one word to focus on for an entire year. A word to challenge that part of my temperament where some kind of change and renewal were needed to enrich my life and transform my character. The word that "fell" upon my heart after a few days of contemplation and prayer was "patience;" definitely-not-at-all the word I wanted to hear.

Patience takes forbearance, tolerance, composure, perseverance, calmness, and tenacity, which meant I would have to learn to tolerate the times of waiting, delay, and trouble in my life with a calm state of mind instead of becoming angry and upset. My entire disposition in everything would need to transform and change, and that was a very tall order!

I knew God was truly speaking to my heart, for when I took a deep and humble look within, I could find no sign of a patient person residing there. But I was committed to take this challenge, and I spent not only one, but two years of focus, on this truly inspiring and life changing word called patience.

While I focused to notice all the areas in life that require patience, I found that everything in life requires a vast amount of patience! Patience with ourselves, patience with others; patience while we wait and patience as we go; patience in our faith, as we wait for God's direction and answers to our prayers.

Today, I can honestly say how glad I am that I chose to embrace this journey in patience, for it has been one of the most fulfilling challenges I have ever endeavored. Patience truly changes everything, inside and out, and has transformed my life in the most amazing ways.

Accepting and embracing patience as our ally and not our enemy will set us free from living a life in constant frustration and anxiety. Patience opens doors to see all the wonderful things that life sets before us, as we cease to be blinded by our constant impatience.

Patience isn't always easy by any means, but nothing good ever comes from living life effortlessly. When we accept patience as our friend and not the enemy it's often portrayed to be, our lives will be set free from the constant frustration and anxiety that comes when we are impatient.

Patience nurtures tolerance, persistence, and trust when we let it permeate deep within our thoughts and hearts, and will change and renew every part of you, bringing with it a life full of more peace, calmness, and compassion for others.

The journey in patience is well worth the taking, for it brings the greatest change of character by bringing a new insight to everything. Patience allows us to see things more clearly with renewed understanding and is the foundation of all good things in life, including love, hope, and even Faith. Learn to be patient with yourself first and your journey will grow from there, for every good change and transformation begins from within and will work its way outward to reach every place in your life that needs more patience.

feeling stuck? step out.

"The thief comes only to steal and kill and destroy;
I came that they may have life, and have it to the full [abundantly]."

John 10:10 NIV

Getting "UN" Stuck

We all get stuck at times in our lives, thinking there has to be something else, something more, something better. Those times that little voice in our heads keeps nudging us in the back of our minds, saying to us that this can't possibly be all that there is!

We can see all of the wonderful possibilities and opportunities that life has to offer, so we bravely ask ourselves... Where do I begin? Yet, this one crucial question comes with no easy answers but only more questions to ponder; such as how can I, how do I, I don't think I'm good enough. These questions that lead to such overwhelming fear, doubt and confusion, leaving us feeling even more stuck and defeated than we were to begin with.

We then listen to the lies in our heads to justify that we're "OK", by using every excuse we can think of and telling ourselves that we just need to find a way to be happy in this place that we currently live in. We try to convince ourselves that things could be worse, it's just a slump, life isn't that bad, and this too shall pass. The cycle continues and always will, until we make a different choice to take that first vulnerable step that will free us from this stagnant place that we are stuck in.

Choosing to settle in this motionless place for too long will only create regrets that we'll be sorry for later, while allowing opportunities to pass by us that may never come around again. God is always opening a new door for us, but if we don't walk through the threshold, the door may end up closed forever.

Getting unleashed from our current situation will require change, and change can bring uncertainty and fear. I truly believe it is these two very things that are the reason we get stuck in the first place. Change brings second chances, opportunities, and new paths to embark upon, giving us renewed energy, determination, and a goal to strive for. Change is good, change is your friend, and when you begin to understand it as such, you will be taking that first step out of your rut.

God didn't create us for only one stationary purpose. He placed us here to learn and grow all through our journeys. He wants abundance and joy for us while we travel life's paths, and it is up to us to do our part to receive this wonderful promise from him.

When I find myself stuck and unsettled, I know that God is nudging me to take the next step of purpose in my journey. I open my eyes, ears, and heart, to see all He is revealing, and stand on the beautiful promise He gives to all of us in Proverbs 3:5-6 "trust in the Lord with all your heart and lean not on your own understanding; in all your ways submit to Him, and He will make your paths straight" (NIV).

Step out of that place that is holding you hostage so that you can begin to find the answer to that initial question; Yes, there is always more waiting for you and God will lead you into the next leg of your journey.

let go. heal. renew.

"Be completely humble and gentle; be patient, bearing with one another in love."

Ephesians 4:2

Restoring Broken Trust

Relationships are built on trust, that firm belief we have in one another that makes us feel safe, bonded, and secure with each other. And just as we need trust in our relationship with God, we also need to be able to trust the people He places within our lives.

Trust is the foundation of any relationship, and many times that trust can be tested, tried and even broken when we choose to be untruthful, or walk away from that person who truly needs our support and was totally depending on us.

The times we find out that we've been lied to, the situations that reveal a truth that was never known to us, or when we discover that something we believed was never real, are just a few of the circumstances that can break the bonds of trust.

All that we felt so confident and assured in is now being questioned, swallowed up in doubt, confusion, and hurt. We feel wounded and betrayed, so we put up walls to protect ourselves, walls to keep out others that "might" shatter our trust again, believing that this is the way to never be hurt again.

My first marriage ended because of adultery, and adultery robs you of every bit of trust that you ever had. The person you "trusted" with every part of your being has broken every strand of that chord that you believed was so tightly woven. If they could do this to you then anyone could, and not only do you lose trust in everyone else, you also lose trust in yourself; your judgement, perspective, and all you held precious.

Yet, if we allow those who have broken our trust to consume our minds with fear and apprehension, telling ourselves that no one is trustworthy, we eventually close ourselves off from everyone.

This wall we build will cause more damage than good, for not only does this fortress keep out that which "might" harm us again, it blocks off the opportunity to heal, move on and trust once again.

So how do we regain trust in our lives once again after it has been washed away? It's a choice we make to walk through forgiveness, let go of what hurt us and ask God for His healing hand in each situation that harmed us, so that we can open our hearts to trust again.

When trust is broken blatantly & intentionally we still must forgive to move on, and this kind of broken trust will sever a relationship forever. Most of the time when trust is broken it's not done from a place of personal intention to harm another, but more likely than not it comes from a place of unspoken expectations, misunderstandings, and lack of selfless understanding.

Regaining trust to restore the relationships with those who have harmed or broken that bond takes an open and honest conversation, time for the hurt to heal and patience to rebuild that trust again. Once we can understand the reasons that caused our trust to become detached, we can work towards restoring that relationship that once was broken.

always be true to you

"I praise you because I am fearfully and wonderfully made;
your works are wonderful, I know that full well."

Psalm 139:14 NIV

Know Your True "You"

What would you say if I asked you the question "Who are you?"

You most likely would start with your name and go on from there to share what you do; I'm a doctor, a writer, a clerk, a teacher…whatever title that job has given you to define the purpose designated to you in your career. As we continue on in our conversation, you may share that you're a mother/father, daughter/son, sister/brother, or husband/wife — the "life" roles that God has blessed you with and assigned you to carry out.

And yes, you may hold one or more of these wonderful life positions, but are they really who you truly are, or more of "what" you do that defines who you are in the outside world, and not the person who lives deep within.

When I was in counseling while going through the divorce of my first marriage, my counselor asked me this very question; "Who are you; who is Sue?" Well I was completely stumped and at a loss for words (which hardly ever happens to me of all people), with no answer at all to offer her, for I never had truly thought about this. Right now, I could only see myself as a person getting a divorce and no longer a wife. Yes, I was also a daughter, sister, friend, and a hairstylist, the wonderful roles God had blessed me with, but all I could see was that I was a person with way too much to deal with who had lost her true self.

As I took some time to really think about this and come up with an answer to her question for our next session, I began to understand that all of these things that described "who" I was, only explained "where" I was in my life at that moment, and began to realize that who we truly are goes well beyond the individual roles we play or the various titles we hold.

First and most importantly, I am God's creation; a human being intricately woven together with unique thoughts, feelings, dreams, desires, and gifts that lay the foundation of who "I" truly am. I am the person lovingly chosen by God who was created in His image with His unconditional love for a significant purpose in His divine plan.

I am loved, I am giving, I am sensitive, I am passionate. I feel things more deeply, I fight harder, I persevere longer, and I overthink everything. All of these things are what make me who I truly am, the qualities, features and traits that God designed me with and are what shape me into the true "me" I am deep within. The unique pieces of me that affect all that I do; the choices I make, the emotions I feel, and the values that are so important to me, all begin with first knowing the person God initially created me to be.

Every additional role, purpose, and opportunity that comes into our lives along the way are based on this foundation, this person who is fearfully and wonderfully created by the loving hands of God.

let's talk!

"Be completely humble and gentle, be patient, bearing with one another in love."

Ephesians 4:2 NIV

Expectations Need a Voice

Expectations are the thoughts we hold in our mind and beliefs we keep in our heart, assuming that whatever we want, desire, and "expect" to happen somehow magically will.

We expect our spouses to buy us that perfect gift, presume others will always understand us enough to know just what we need and when, while we surmise that those who are closest to us and know us best will somehow read our minds and hearts to satisfy our every expectation.

And the crazy thing is, we expect these things to materialize, in spite of the fact that we have never asked or even had a conversation to discuss or share the things we need, hope and long for with the person we expect to fulfill them.

How can we possibly think or believe that any expectation can ever be met if we keep them silently hidden within, never to let anyone in on our secret needs and all the things we want to happen.

For many years in my marriage I assumed that if my husband loved me enough he should just know the greatest inclinations of my heart and the deepest yearnings within my soul, for if he didn't, well then, he truly didn't know me or love me at all.

After years of being disappointed and hurt, because that is exactly what happens when expectations aren't met, I began to realize what a ridiculous and ludicrous thought process this actually was.

How was my husband, or anyone else for that matter, supposed to know my favorite color, flower, or my innermost wishes, if I never spoke of them and just kept them hidden within myself with no attempt to let them out? If I never shared any of this information with anyone, how could they possibly know? And even if my husband tried to read my heart, his assumptions would most likely be wrong and cause even more damage, to no fault of his own.

Granted, there are certain expectations in life that don't always require a "voice": the expectations that hold us accountable to ourselves and each other, such as being trustworthy, truthful, respectful, and kind. The morals and values that hold us responsible to be a righteous person and live a life of integrity are something we all expect from one another.

But every other expectation must be given a voice, in a conversation, a message or some form of communication, for if not, we will always end up hurt and discouraged, while building a wall of frustration and anger between ourselves and others. We certainly cannot assume that someone else should just know what we need, want, or expect, if we haven't shared any of these secret desires with them.

Jesus tells us that God will give us all we need for our joy to be complete, but we must "ask" for these things in Jesus name first. So if God wants us to ask for all we need from Him, why would we believe it should be any different for us to do the same with one another?

Give your expectations a voice with love and respect, while clearly laying out those needs and desires you hold in your heart, and open that door of opportunity for yourself and others, while avoiding any unnecessary illusions that will cause only heartache and disappointment.

embrace the vulnerable within

"But he said to me, 'My grace is sufficient for you, for my power is made perfect in weakness.' Therefore, I will boast all the more gladly about my weaknesses, so that Christ's power may rest on me."

2 Corinthians 12:9 NIV

Embracing Your Vulnerability

When you look up the definition of "vulnerable", you will find words such as hopelessness, weakness, and defenselessness. The emotions and feelings we all have at times, the ones we're ashamed of and hide from not only ourselves but others as well.

Yet I believe our vulnerable side is a beautiful piece of who we genuinely are; that special delicate place within our hearts that keeps us humble and true to ourselves and God. That space within that leaves more room for Him to come intimately closer to us as he gently whispers how much He loves us, when we find ourselves in the vulnerable places of fear, unworthiness, and helplessness.

When we embrace our vulnerability, we open a door to be set free from whatever it is we're ashamed of, and whatever it is we're ignoring and running from. Vulnerability brings truth to those delicate places within and allows God to do His greatest work in us, when we take off the masks we've been hiding behind and learn to love every part of ourselves.

I have had anxiety most of my life, which manifests many frightening and fragile emotions, such as panic, doubt, worry, and fear. People perceived me as strong and yet had no idea how truly fragile I was deep inside, because I wouldn't allow myself to be vulnerable enough to share this truth with anyone, not even myself.

I was ashamed, I didn't want to disappoint anyone, and I certainly didn't want to admit that "I" needed help and someone else to be strong for me sometimes. This charade that I tried so hard to uphold took over my life with bitterness, hurt and anger, and caused me to lose myself while damaging many of my relationships with others. Any time we try to cover up the weaker side of us, we tend to go to the opposite extreme of what we are truly feeling, and that place will only exasperate even more of what we're trying to hide from.

And then one day as my daughter and I were sitting out on the patio, she looked directly at me and said, "Mom, you need to learn to be vulnerable." It always amazes me how God brings truth through those whom He knows will get our best attention,, and I heard loud and clear what He was saying to me that day.

Embracing my vulnerability has truly set me free, for I no longer have to hide, put on a fake face, or feel that I'm less of person when those times of anxiety appear out of nowhere. I'm free to be me, and there is nothing more liberating than that.

Free yourself to be the complete person you are, weaknesses and all, by embracing every beautiful piece of yourself...especially your vulnerable side!

I am yours

"For whoever wants to save their life will lose it, but whoever loses their life for me will find it."

Matthew 19:25 NIV

I Belong to Jesus

What does it mean when we truly surrender all we are to Jesus?

Surrendering is defined as "giving up" something, and we have a difficult time doing that, don't we? We may feel like we're quitting, losing, or succumbing to failure, when we try to give up anything.

But surrendering to Jesus is none of these things; it is a freedom that comes from "releasing" all of the things that hold us back and keep us in a place that will eventually defeat us.

Doubt, worry, fear, and more come from holding onto the things we can't possibly know or control, keeping us chained to a wall that leads to nowhere. When we depend on ourselves and the world to hold us up, we will always feel unfulfilled, dissatisfied, and "out of control": losing the very things we're trying so hard to hold onto.

But when we "release" our hearts, our thoughts, and our lives to Him, we set ourselves free to allow His love and Spirit to become a part of who we are.

When I chose to walk my life in Faith, I made a commitment to Jesus to do my best to follow Him and live according to God's will for my life. It is a daily decision to continue to renew this commitment, for life will always bring its distractions, and Satan will try even harder to mess things up as we draw closer to Jesus, because Satan doesn't want anyone giving more of themselves to God. But, when you have Jesus as your "number one," nothing in life will be able to defeat you or hold you back!

Surrendering to Jesus gives us a partner, and no longer do we have to do anything alone, carry our burdens by ourselves, fear the unknown or depend on anyone or anything else to fulfill us.

Giving our lives to Jesus allows His light from within us to radiate His love into the world and onto others. This light that will also illuminate a new path for us, with a clearer purpose and renewed perspective.

Giving ourselves to Jesus doesn't cause us to lose anything at all and quite to the contrary, it gives us so much more. As we let go all of that we've have been holding onto for so long, we make room for Him in our hearts and souls, to fill and fulfill us in ways that nothing else can.

Our lives take on a whole new meaning when we choose to submit and follow Him: when we choose to live life with the Spirit within as our foundation and are no longer led by only the desires of our flesh (human ways).

We become a branch to His vine, being fully nurtured by the only One who can supply us with all we will ever need, in ways that only Jesus can.

pushing simple

"Blessed is the one who perseveres under trial because, having stood the test, that person will receive the crown of life that the Lord has promised to those who love him."

James 1:12 NIV

Nothing Good Comes from Easy

Most of us tend to look for those "easy" buttons in life, that path that takes the smallest amount of effort and work to get us from point A to Z. We seek the quickest and least demanding way to go when trying to find avenues and answers to accomplish whatever it is we are aiming to achieve.

We live in a society that demands instant gratification, from one thing to another, believing that "easy" is the thing to always strive for to find our way in and out of everything. We become impatient in every challenging situation, only seeking that easy way out, ending up making our circumstances even more difficult than they were when they began, for our expectation of easy never quite works out as easily as we think it should have.

I think of Jesus and His walk on earth and how nothing was ever easy for him. But there was a reason and purpose for his challenging journey, which would have turned out completely different for both him and us, had it been trouble-free and simple.

You see, easy doesn't really accomplish anything except to make life less fulfilling. Every challenge in life builds patience, perseverance, and character, while leading us to a place of greater fulfillment in growth and purpose than any *undemanding* way ever could.

When we focus on easy, we shut out all else that God is working in and around us and miss the whole big picture, for all we see is the immediate snapshot in front of us.

Easy buttons tend to bring regrets and wishful do-overs in those times we look back and think we've completed our mission, only to realize we should of, could of, or would have done it better, if we only had taken the time to look past that tempting easy way in or out.

I'm not saying that everything in life should be difficult, but we should try to look beyond that instant gratification and desire to take more time to think things through before always reaching for that initial "easy button."

When we stop for a moment to explore every option and allow ourselves time to pay more attention to all the possible answers available, we can achieve the best outcome in all situations.

God does His greatest work in us, for us and through us when we are willing to step up and do what's right and not just what's easy. I like to say, "do your part with your best effort and God will do the rest." God never promised a life without trials and tribulations; in fact, Jesus told us we would face many challenges, but He did promise to walk with us all along the way.

The next time you find yourself reaching for that "easy" button, take a deep breath and a patient step back. Trust in the process, while leisurely walking along the longer path with eyes fully open to all that surrounds you in order to see life's complete picture, before you make any hasty, easy decisions.

looking beyond

"And we know that in all things God works for the good of those who love him, who have been called according to his purpose."

Romans 8:28 NIV

From One Purpose to Another

We all search for our purpose in life. That one thing that defines who we are, in what we do. The part of life that gives us significance and allows us to prove to the world that we matter and are here for a reason.

Some seek their purpose in a job or career path that rewards them with a paycheck and a title. Others give their lives to a mission, a calling beyond any "normal" expectation that takes them to places many of us would never think of going. Some give their lives for the sake of serving others, with humbleness and sacrifice.

Yet, when we truly look at our lives, we all have more than "one" mission to live, beginning with our foundational basis in purpose beyond ourselves. Those that are mother's and father's have purpose in raising and nurturing a family. A husband and wife have the purpose of investing in a life together. Being a friend has a purpose in love and support for one another. These purposes already add up to more than one!

As life changes, so does our purpose. One purpose may lead to a new objective or goal that will change our existing purpose into a new endeavor, leading us to a new calling that will take that "one" onto a new and even greater adventure.

Some of us may stay longer in one place of purpose, others may have a highway of many twists and turns, with numerous transitions. Either way, our purpose(s) become defined by the places we are called to and the opportunities we choose to open ourselves up to, as life constantly fluctuates and changes direction. Purposes change, grow and become more, in every step along life's paths.

Our significance in life should not come from one single vision we place upon ourselves to define who we are and why we are here. When we believe we were created for only one purpose, we will establish a life of limited fulfillment, missing the chance to be the more that God created us for. Life offers us numerous beautiful opportunities to travel a wonderful journey, with more than only one purpose, at any one given time.

God made each of us with unique and individual gifts, talents, and capabilities. His intention and purpose in our creation was never to limit us to just "one" of anything. He wants us to have a life of abundance, a life filled with plenty, which comes when we expand our vision and purpose beyond one single vocation or calling.

Life is a journey, filled with many paths of purpose. Each purpose touches another, for ourselves as well as others. We were created "on" purpose, for a life full of numerous opportunities! Embrace EVERY purpose life offers to you and may your "one" become "many" as you find your Plural Purpose.

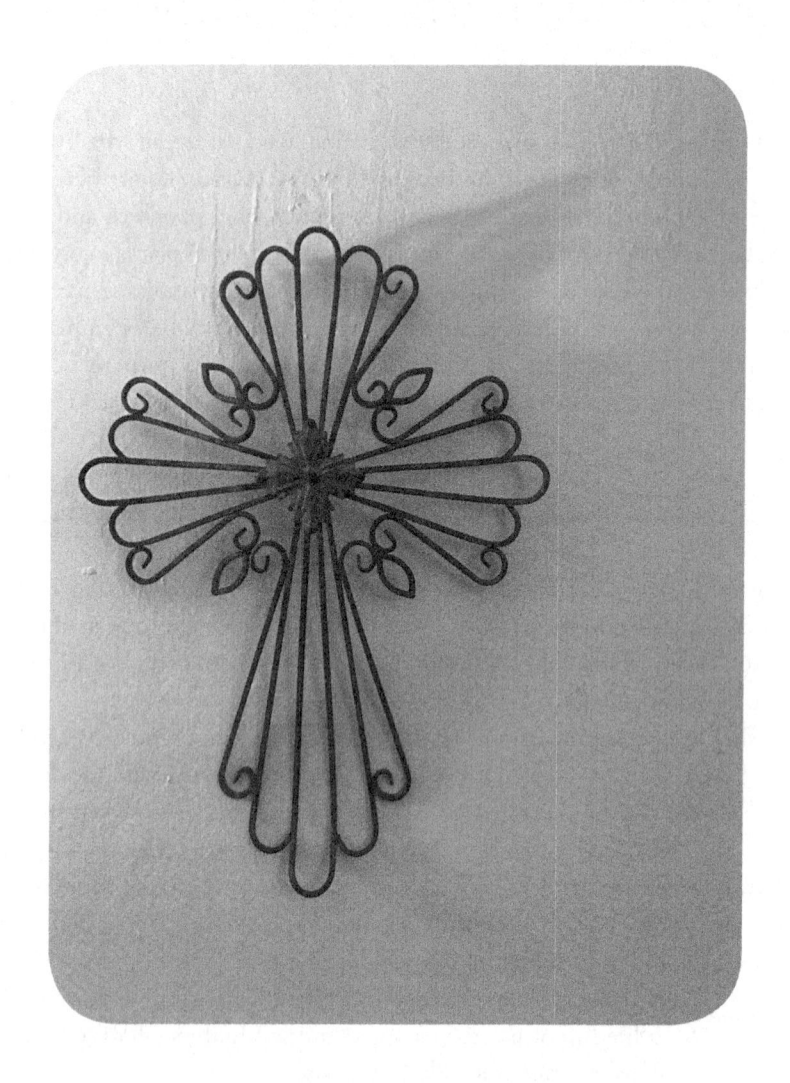

God knows the best way

"The mind governed by the flesh is death,
but the mind governed by the Spirit is life and peace."

Romans 8:6 NIV

Place God in the Center of Every Passionate Endeavor

Our passions keep our lives brilliant and vibrant. Those things we believe in and stand up for with every part of our being that give our lives a greater sense of purpose.

It may be a cause we're fighting for, a goal we're pursuing, a principal we're trying to uphold, a desire to prove truth in an unfair situation, or a compelling need to step up for someone who can't stand up for themselves.

There is nothing wrong in defending our beliefs, morals and values, but sometimes we can get in trouble when our feelings take the driver's seat and we become overly excited about anything.

Our initial driving desire to make a change, a difference, or achieve that goal can become so consumed with our own emotions, thoughts and opinions, that we lose all sense of reasoning and logical thinking.

Anytime we act from a place of total emotion, we can be left with regrets, hurts, and even a tarnished reputation, resulting in an outcome that causes more harm than good to the circumstances at hand.

I am a very transparent and emotional person. When it comes to matters of the heart, I am always willing to jump in and stand up for what I believe in. Yet, what I have come to learn over the years through my own passionate endeavors (and many consequences from being overly enthusiastic) is that before I take action in any situation, I must allow my emotions and logic to meet each other in the middle, by taking it first to God.

I ask God if the passion is something He placed in my heart. If His answer is yes, I quiet those emotions in the best way that I can, while I wait in faithful patience for His wisdom and direction, before I take any first step.

As I move forward in pursuing this passion within, I continue to keep God in that center, to stay humble and true in its purpose and not get lost in myself.

God loves a passionate heart and wants us to stand up for what's right for ourselves, others, and every good cause, but we must do so with balance, God's direction, and a heart open to see beyond just emotion.

Placing God in the center of all our passions will always insure the best outcome in any worthwhile endeavor we find ourselves called to uphold and take part in.

The next time your heart is filled with a passion of purpose, invite God in to discern its full objective, taking His lead and direction to give that passion the best voice possible and most righteous path to follow.

celebrate

"...and that you may love the Lord your God, listen to his voice, and hold fast to him. For the Lord is your life, and he will give you many years in the land he swore to give to your fathers, Abraham, Isaac and Jacob."

Deuteronomy 30:20 NIV

Each Year Is a Gift

Each year that I am blessed to celebrate another year of life, I look back and reflect on the years that have passed; all that they brought, what I have learned, how I have changed, and the blessings that God has so lovingly bestowed upon me. And though some years have been harder to go through than others, I can honestly say that the journey thus far has been amazing!

Could I have made better choices and done some things differently; of course, we can all say that after each life experience, but those choices that could have been different or better are all part of our beautiful life journey that paint a bigger picture of the true testimony to this wonderful gift that God gives to each of us. He combines every year that we travel through and continues to intricately mold and shape us into the more of who He created us to be, to serve a greater purpose in our lives for Him and the world we live in.

I am grateful for every year that adds another number to my journey and honestly wouldn't change a single thing. The moments of joy, the moments of pain, the moments of challenge and struggles have all led me to be right where I am and formed me into who I've become. Each year gives me a clearer perspective in purpose and brings more gratefulness to a heart that has so much to be thankful for, and as I get older, I cherish the little things more, hold onto the memories even tighter, and look forward to seeing how God will continue to use me along the rest of my journey here.

Each year is a gift that leaves its own special legacy to be carried into the next year of life, each year builds upon the last and brings more to our lives than we had before. We gain wisdom and knowledge with each year that passes, as we learn from the mistakes that we no longer have to repeat, and our priorities change as we begin to realize what is truly important in life. Many times it is not until we've accumulated these years under our belt that we are fully prepared for our true purpose, because we needed to *live* more of life to get there!

Don't let that *age number* diminish your purpose, steal your hope, or stop you from living, for God doesn't quit "us" when we reach a certain number, nor should we ever give up on ourselves.

Follow your heart, pursue your passions, age gracefully with love for who you are, and always be grateful for each year of your life journey, as you follow God's never-ending purpose for you.

peace out

"Forget the former things; do not dwell on the past. See, I am doing a new thing!
Now it springs up; do you not perceive it?
I am making a way in the wilderness and streams in the wasteland."

Isaiah 43:18-19 NIV

When it's "Okay" to Walk Away

Do you ever find yourself in a place or situation where you've done all you can, yet things are not changing for better or worse?

It may be that promotion you've been trying so hard to receive at your job, yet the opportunity continues to pass you by only to be offered to someone else. It may be a situation you are in with a friend or family member that is stuck at an impasse, because they can't move beyond a past hurt or misunderstanding. It could be a church or a group you attend that changes direction and no longer serves a purpose in your spiritual journey.

There will be many times throughout our lives when we will have to make a choice as to whether we stay in a certain situation, or decide that it's time to walk away. These are the moments you experience that tug at your heart, when God is telling you it's time to let go and move on from where you currently are, whether you are ready or not.

As life changes we must change as well, and many times, what may have been good for us before, is not so anymore. Doors continually open while others abruptly shut, and each door gives us a way in, as well as a way out.

Many times, God calls us to vacate a place in our lives that no longer serves any purpose for Him, ourselves, or others. We can't continue to carry around all that we accumulate in life, without being weighed down with so much past baggage, leaving no room for new growth and new opportunities. Nor can we stay in situations that leave us feeling hopeless, helpless, and frustrated, when we know that we've done all we can and there is nothing more that we can do. We must learn to let go of what was, and trust God in what is yet to come, knowing He has a greater plan for us.

The most difficult part of walking away from anything is questioning whether you truly did your best and tried hard enough. If you're anything like me, you may find yourself experiencing guilt, because you believe that walking away is somehow quitting or giving up, when it is truly not. Walking away from certain things is a necessary part of life, in order to keep on growing and moving forward along the path that God sets before us.

When you find God calling you to leave something behind, embrace all the good in the blessings that this season has brought to your life and the lessons that it has taught you, leaving no room for sadness, bitterness, or regret, as you find a new direction with peace in your heart to boldly step forward onto the new path that God is preparing for you.

Begin today, to humbly search your heart and soul to find those places in your life that are calling you to make a change. Ask God for His wisdom, lean on His understanding, and find your strength in Him, to gracefully let go of whatever it is that is holding you back, as you move forward to the next step of your journey.

life's best investment

"Two are better than one, because they have a good return for their labor: if either of them falls down, one can help the other up. But pity anyone who falls and has no one to help them up. Also, if two lie down together, they will keep warm. But how can one keep warm alone? Though one may be overpowered, two can defend themselves. A cord of three strands is not quickly broken."

Ecclesiastes 4:9-12 NIV

Marriage—Life's Best Investment

Marriage is an investment in a relationship where we commit to devote our time, effort, energy and ourselves to the greatest life partnership we will ever have. It is a choice that joins two people together as one as a team to travel together along life's journey with love, support and companionship.

When God created Adam and Eve, He created marriage knowing that two are stronger than one, and each one can be better with the other. Marriage allows us to share our life joys, pains, and everything in-between, making the good times better and the hardships more bearable when we have that partner to walk with and lean on.

We invest our money in savings accounts, stock portfolios and IRA's to protect and grow them into more. In the same way, we must invest ourselves into our marriages to keep them healthy, stable, and secure.

Yet, marriage seems to be the most vulnerable and neglected relationship of all. There are no schools that offer marriage degrees, no step-by-step instruction manuals to tell us exactly how to "do marriage". We find our significant other, get married, start a family, and continue on with our jobs, careers and all else that life offers us, while assuming that our marriage will just take care of itself, and many times it is not our first priority, but sadly, our last.

While we are investing ourselves in all of these other priorities, which can certainly leave us overwhelmed and exhausted, we find ourselves with nothing left at all to give or put into our marriage. A marriage requires the investment of time, effort, and discipline with love, selflessness, compassion, humility and understanding, to give it the chance it deserves to thrive and survive.

Marriage is a gift from God to cherish and nurture. We make a vow to not only each other but to Him as well, when we stand before our Loving Father and promise ourselves to each other. The down payment is the vow and promise. The return we receive on our marriage investment will depend on how many installments we deposit along its journey, and just as with any investment, the more you put it, the more your investment will grow, and the more you will reap and receive.

The union of two people committing to "do" life together is truly the greatest gift that God offers us, through the blessings that come from investing ourselves and hearts to another with God at the center to form a bond that is stronger than any other.

...not yet

"Desire without knowledge is not good—how much more will hasty feet miss the way!"

Proverbs 19:2 NIV

Wait! Don't Jump Just Yet!

Do you ever find yourself "jumping" from one thing to the next...taking leaps and bounds to the point of pure confusion and utter exhaustion?

Something changes, something ends, something takes an unexpected turn, and all you want to do is jump on over to the next thing to keep moving forward, never stopping to look back at what exactly just happened.

Well, life truly doesn't work out that well when we immediately "jump" from one thing to the next, if we don't stop to take a breather and reflect on what that last step just brought, before being able to see what the next step even looks like.

Each ending or change that comes our way leaves us with something to learn, digest, or work through, allowing us to then see more clearly that next bridge we need to cross over to continue our journey. When we lose someone dear to us, we must grieve first in order to heal. A lost relationship has many feelings to mend before we can be emotionally whole to move on to another. A mistake or bad choice requires some soul searching and change in perspective to keep us from another hasty or erroneous decision. All we go through in life must first find its own peace, purpose and closure before we are able to see the next window of opportunity.

As we step back, before we act or react, and "wait" for a moment or two instead of quickly "jumping" into our next venture, we allow God the opportunity to make good out of each situation, letting Him prepare us for whatever comes next.

He will offer you wisdom and guidance, heal your hurt, and reveal a new and better direction, as He holds your hand and speaks to your heart while you "wait." He will make your weak places stronger, lessen your fears, and prepare you for what lies ahead, when you choose to be patient and give Him the time do exactly that.

If we are always in such a hurry to quickly jump forward to what lies directly in front of us, we lose sight of the complete picture as to what life truly has to offer us. We forget that there is a power greater than us, a God who stands beside us and wants to travel with us, helping us with every new step to be the best one yet.

Every step that we take and each life circumstance we meet are building blocks that make us stronger and wiser in order to create a more stable foundation. While we hold back our instant urge to jump, we can see how one brick stacks on top of the other to build and support a solid life structure.

Life is a journey of many steps with detours, obstacles, and mountains that sometimes appear out of nowhere. But if we can just have a little patience and resist the urge to hastily jump from one thing to another without any thought as to where we've just come from, we will receive so much more to be fully fit and ready to leap into that next life step of opportunity.

make today your best yesterday

"This is the day the Lord has made; let us rejoice and be glad in it."

Psalm 118:24 ESV

Make Today Your Best Yesterday

Each day at midnight, what was known as today evolves into what we will now refer to as yesterday.

Our yesterdays create beautiful memories and design our life journal, but sometimes they leave behind pain and regrets when we continue to carry the things we need to work through and let go of into our new todays and tomorrows.

How often do we find ourselves missing all the new day before us will bring, because we carry over what troubled us most from the yesterday that is no longer?

A problem with no solution yet, a situation that causes hurt feelings or anger to linger, or a circumstance that came unexpectedly and left us with a change of direction or new challenge to face. The times we wake up with too many leftovers from the day left behind and forget that today is a new gift of opportunity to begin creating another beautiful yesterday for your life journey.

When we get stuck in all that happened in our yesterday, we can miss many of the wonderful things that today is bringing us.

Each day of our life has its own reason and purpose as one day leads to another, giving us daily gifts in lessons, direction, blessings, and all we need to keep creating new and better tomorrows.

I like to look at each new day as an empty box to fill up, a new beginning for the rest of my life and another chance to create the "best yesterday" in the now of today.

Do I want to carry over all the stress, worry and fear, feeling stuck and not able to move on to the new day before me? Or do I choose to take what yesterday left me with as a gift to my future?

Yes, life is ever changing and will always have its situations and issues, but we have free will to choose what we place in our new box of today.

We can choose to carry forward all that makes us stronger and wiser, while holding onto the memories that brought us a smile, or we can choose to keep bringing along that which no longer serves a purpose and only gets in the way of the new day before us.

The choice we make will not only direct the course of the new day ahead of us but will also influence our focus on all of the things that this new day is offering to us.

Whatever your yesterday brought to you, hold on to the good and let go of the rest while trusting God to take any of those frustrating "leftovers" to transform each day into something new and better, so you can clearly see this present day as the gift that it is…a fresh new start in life to create an even better yesterday.

When we look at life in this way, we will always be striving to live each of our days to their fullest potential, while completing another wonderful page to add to our life's journal of the best yesterday's ever.

we are all connected

"And let us consider how we may spur one another on toward love and good deeds,
not giving up meeting together, as some are in the habit of doing,
but encouraging one another—and all the more as you see the Day approaching."

Hebrews 10:24-25 NIV

Relationship Connects Us

Life and all its being begins with relationship, the connection we have with God, each other, and all that exists around us.

Relationship is the parallel bond that we live in together, that which makes us stronger, unites us, and enables us to be a true presence with a greater purpose for the world that we live in and God's divine plan for all of us.

We were not created to be alone in this vast space we reside in, for God created each of us to be intertwined with one another. We are truly all related, born from God's initial human creation: the place where it all started with one man and one woman, the place where the miracle of procreation began and continues to multiply over and over.

We may think of relationships as only the intimate bonds that we share with family and friends, those whom we are more intricately connected to through blood relationships and close friendships. And although this is true, we must also realize that relationship goes well beyond these personal bonds. We relate to others in so many ways that we don't always see as relationship at all…ways we don't notice or even pay enough attention to think about but yet are so very important.

We are divinely bonded to that stranger on the street, the person standing in line with us, and every other single human being that we encounter. God lives in each of us and the greatest way He reaches us is through another person. Each time God places someone in our paths, He connects us for reasons that may be quite obvious to us, as well as many that we will never see or understand, but each one holds their own value in some way, for one or both of us.

Life is all about relationship, the basis of all that is precious, both human and spiritual. As we see ourselves as a part of one another, we come to realize that this connection is more significant and extraordinary than any other.

We must gain a higher awareness as to how important relationship is and always be mindful to offer respect, compassion, and understanding to every person God places along our path…for this is how God fulfills His plan and purpose for each of our lives. Through this vast connection in a world full of billions of people, it is through relationship that He meets our needs, fulfills our dreams, and brings us together in perfect timing.

This union, this bond, to God and each other is what keeps us awake in a life that goes well beyond ourselves, as we travel through this world together.

keep walking. keep believing.

"Even though I walk through the darkest valley, I will fear no evil, for you are with me; your rod and staff, they comfort me."

Psalm 23:4 NIV

Fear and Faith

Do you ever question your faith when you feel afraid? I think we are led to believe that when we fear, our faith is weak.

We live in an imperfect world, and this world can be quite a scary place. So many disturbing things constantly happening that bring great distress, worry, and fear.

Fear is a human emotion and it serves its own purpose, to help us determine what is safe and what is not, but it can also become quite overwhelming when what we fear makes us feel weak, especially when it comes to our faith.

God tells us to "fear not" and to trust Him in all things, but He also understands our "human side" and uses our fears to come closer to us. He knows we will face troubles in this world that will bring anguish to our souls and will test our trust and belief in Him, as well as ourselves; and these are the times He will carry us in His loving arms, as we walk through those fearful places we find ourselves in.

Each year when I schedule my annual mammogram, no matter how hard I try to not be afraid, I am still filled with fear because of all the what if's and unknowns that scare me to death, for I once had to go through a biopsy procedure that frightened me in ways I had never experienced before.

And although I consider myself a person of great faith, I still fear this exam every year. The fear while I wait for the result and all that result "might" bring, that could turn my whole life upside-down in a moment, and then be changed forever. I know deep in my heart that God will be with me to bring me through anything, but I still feel afraid of all those "What If" possibilities, and then feel ashamed and condemned because my faith wasn't strong enough to take away those fears that paralyze me.

But then I realize that even Jesus was afraid when He knew His death was inevitable. He shed fearful tears and even pleaded with God for a different outcome, as he prayed in the garden before He was crucified. When Jesus was human, he too felt this same emotion, and He too was afraid; and I don't think that any one of us would question the Faith of Jesus, yet we do exactly that to ourselves.

Fear doesn't make our faith weaker, it makes it that much stronger, for as we walk in our fear, we grasp onto our faith that much harder. Our faith holds us up and supports us; our faith sustains our trust and belief in Him.

Fear will always exist in our world here, and God will always be by our side with more faith to offer us, as we walk through those frightening places that tempt to scare the faith out of us.

transformation

"Not only so, but we also glory in our sufferings, because we know that suffering produces perseverance; perseverance, character; and character, hope."

Romans 5:3-4 NIV

Scars Are Stars of Resilience

We all carry scars; the reminders of life's most difficult places along our journeys that tried to completely break and beat us down forever.

Scars usually bring memories of hurt and pain, because a scar is formed only after we have suffered through something that has deeply wounded us, either physically or emotionally.

Most people see a scar as something ugly, a permanent, unpleasing mark on one's body or invisible wound to the heart that we attach weakness or sadness to, but once you look past the surface of any scar there is a beauty behind every scar's remarkable story when embraced and recognized for the strength, restoration, and healing that it truly represents.

I look at scars as a beautiful reminder of God's love, grace and mercy in our lives. No matter what we've been through, no matter how many scars we've been left with, each scar has its own beautiful testimony as to what we have endured and overcome, as well as a clearer vision to God in our lives and the good that He always brings from every battle, challenge, and storm that we travel through.

Our scars transform us, while building our Faith, trust, and characters, and exemplify a life lived with determination and perseverance. They symbolize strength for all the times we never gave up when we stumbled and fell, but always chose to endure and get back on our feet to keep moving forward, growing, and becoming a better person...scars and all!

Scars represent how resilient we are, scars bear witness to the trials we've walked in and walked out of, and scars show that our vulnerability made us that much stronger.

Our scars are unique and personal to each of us; every one has a wonderful story to remind us that God is always our strength and will heal whatever damage that life brings our way.

The scars that make us stronger, the scars that teach us valuable lessons, the scars that show us God's amazing power, and the scars that change us into someone better, all remind us of how God can restore and make everything beautiful again.

Scars will never permanently tarnish our life journey, as long as we see that God heals and brings something extraordinary from each scar we've acquired to make our lives shine even brighter.

surrender all to Him

"The Lord will fight for you; you need only to be still."

Exodus 14:14 NIV

It's Not Always Your Battle to Fight

We all face battles at one time or another through the course of our lives. Those times when those more difficult challenges come upon us and test the core of who we are and everything we believe in.

There will be times we feel we must stand up and fight to defend ourselves, those we love, or anything else in our lives that is being threatened and bringing some kind of harm to us.

It may be something we are unfairly being judged in, a rumor that is being spread that holds no truth, or a value we hold so dear that is being attacked and questioned.

Our emotions go into overdrive, we put on our boxing gloves, and are ready to do whatever it takes to defend our beliefs, morals, values, and characters.

Now I'm not saying that there aren't times we need to stand up for certain things in our life, but we must first discern if the battle is worth the fight and whether our plan of attack will cause more harm than good to the situation at hand.

Not too long ago, I found myself in a battle brought on by a group of people in a place where one goes to feel safe and whose foundation is based on God's truth.

I was wrongly accused of things that I never did, based on the lies, gossip, and assumptions of others. The worse thing anyone can do to me is attack my character by spewing lies about me.

This attack came in the form of a letter, and once I read all that it said, I took a deep breath and realized that this battle was not meant for me to fight, so I chose to give it to God and let Him fight for me. I realized that anything I would have said or done would have fueled the fire and caused more harm to me, my family, and friends.

God says He will fight for us in these types of circumstances; He tells us to lay our burdens at His feet, and then walk peacefully away in faith and trust, knowing He will do what is best for us, and that is exactly what He did for me. As I stepped away from everything, I found His peace in my heart as I trusted Him, His strength in my soul to keep moving on with my life, while His protection kept me safe from any further harm.

Whenever we find ourselves in the middle of any battlefield, we must discern what His will is for us in order to truly know whether we need to step up in some way, or step back and allow Him to fight for us.

God always knows more than we do, and His ways will always bring justice, conviction, and healing to those involved in any conflict, to work through whatever He sees as necessary for each person involved in any battle.

the perfect "hand"

"Now to him who is able to do immeasurably more than all we ask or imagine, according to his power that is at work within us."

Ephesians 3:20

God Qualifies Us

Many times, when God calls us to do something we either ignore Him completely or run away shouting no way, no how, not me! No way are we capable enough, good enough, strong enough, or smart enough, but whatever reasons we give ourselves to say that we can't, God has a bigger and better reason to say that we can. He believes in us more than we do in ourselves and always sees a greater potential for us than we can see for ourselves.

God knows our fears, weaknesses, and doubts, but unlike us, He looks at these things as benefits, not as the obstacles we may see them as. He knows our hearts, our circumstances, our challenges, our mistakes, and regrets, and yet He sees what we "can" be, even when we do not. God will never call you to do anything on your own, and He will always equip you with all you need and more to get the job done.

When God first called me to write, I chuckled to myself and said to Him, "You have got to be kidding me, what can I possibly have to share that would make a difference to anyone?" And as usual, when God calls you to something, He doesn't let it go that easily, and the nudge in my heart would not go away. After two weeks I finally said yes to Him, trusting that He would be "my enough," and bring all that I needed and more to do what He was calling me to. I have been writing almost every day since then, as His spirit continues to fill my heart with inspirations to share with others. If I would have listened to myself and all of those "I cannot" doubts in my head and my heart, I would have missed this wonderful adventure and purpose that He had the confidence in me to do, even though I did not.

I believe God calls us to many things that seem impossible and uncomfortable to us, to allow us to grow in faith and trust, so that we can get closer to Him and He can come closer to us, to connect in that personal relationship with Him that makes all the difference in our lives.

It is not the things that we believe we are enough for, it is those that test us, grow us, and transform our characters that will fulfill every purpose God has for our lives and bring the greatest blessings to ourselves and others.

God has a reason in every purpose He calls us to, and you can be assured that He'll give you all that you need to do what He's asking of you.

The next time you feel that nudge, take the plunge, knowing that God is preparing the way for you to succeed in the plan He is calling you to. Then watch His amazing come into your life; I can promise you that when God calls you to it, you will experience one of the most amazing life adventures ever!

room to flow

"Many are the plans in the mind of man,
but it is the purpose of the Lord that will stand."

Proverbs 19:21 ESV

Give Your Life Some "Wiggle" Room!

Our jobs, families, obligations, time to eat, sleep and play, push our lives into a sort of robotic state, leaving no room to "wiggle."

We become so consumed with our daily regimented and organized schedules, filling up every minute to its fullest capacity, that we seem to forget that life needs some flexibility for the "unexpected" surprises that always arise to disrupt our perfect agendas.

The car breaks down, your child gets sick, or a problem arises that needs your immediate attention: these are some of the more frustrating interruptions our days may encounter. Sometimes the interruptions are more pleasant, like when a friend calls with a spontaneous lunch invitation, a door suddenly opens for a long-awaited opportunity, or maybe a plan is abruptly cancelled that allows you some desperately needed room to breathe. These things never happen according to "our" perfect schedules, and whether they are pleasing or not, they can throw us off track when we don't leave some room in our day to wiggle.

Whatever it is, we need to allow freedom to "wiggle," with an accepting and unruffled disposition, for those times when life calls us to go in a different direction.

I used to be quite the control freak, quite honestly. Setting each day up with a list full of things to do and accomplish. And if anything at all disrupted my "perfect" plan, I became annoyed and frustrated, letting it ruin my entire day, even when the interruptions were delightful unexpected blessings.

There is nothing wrong in making plans for your day and trying to follow an organized timetable, we all need that to keep some balance and stability in our lives, but I'm just suggesting that you leave a place in each day to accept the unexpected with an open and willing positive perspective, when life calls you to change direction and step out of your busy schedule.

Many times, we miss God in our lives because we are so consumed focusing on all those things we plan to do and ignore the callings, opportunities, and extra special blessings that He is bringing us. Interruptions have reasons that we may not always see, but God never interrupts us to just waste our time.

I have learned to be okay when these interruptions come into my day and look forward to seeing what God is up to, knowing there is always a blessing, a need being fulfilled, or an unexpected opportunity that God is bringing me to do or receive, and His plans are always so much better than any strategy I could attempt to orchestrate on my own.

When we learn to be flexible, we leave more room for God's amazing presence in our lives, and life is so much better when we leave some room to "wiggle."

let boundaries lead to bridges

"He grants peace to your borders and satisfies you with the finest of wheat."

Psalm 147:14 NIV

Boundaries

We all need to learn how to incorporate healthy boundaries into our lives. Boundaries are necessary to keep order in our lives by making us aware of what has a positive influence on us and what doesn't.

They enable us to stop what is coming in that is harming us, while giving us a way to make the changes we need to bring a better quality to our lives. A boundary can be as small as saying no to someone, or as large as having to completely walk out of a situation.

Though boundaries are often seen as barricades to keep something bad out, they can also be interpreted as bridges to cross over to allow something good to now have room to enter.

Every boundary requires a change of some sort, and change is difficult for most people. Boundaries bring consequential changes to the one setting the boundary, as well as to the one who will have to receive it.

For example, if you are a yes person who is always agreeable to everyone else's everything, you may worry that when you say no to something they need or expect from you, it will cause them to no longer like you and may even stop them from being a part of your life.

Or, if you find yourself in a relationship that causes only pain, frustration, and holds you down, and you need to place a boundary between you and this person by walking away from this situation, you might find that the other person involved is not very accepting of this boundary you have chosen to put up, and they may try to manipulate you with guilt and condemnation to keep you right where you are.

But to say yes when your heart's telling you to say no, and to stay when you know you must go, does nothing good for anyone.

When I went to counseling a few years ago, my counselor told me I had to learn how to place healthy boundaries in my life, in order to heal and move past that which was holding me back.

It takes a special kind of strength to put up these boundaries in our lives, a strength that can only come from God, through the Spirit that lives within us. For, in order for a boundary to be healthy and healing, it must be built with compassion, wisdom, and understanding, and only God can give us all of these things when we decide it's time to place that boundary in our lives.

Boundaries are necessary for protection and healing, and they offer new opportunities, new beginnings, and a new path to continue to travel on that will allow you to continue to grow.

Take these burdensome choices and decisions to God first and allow Him to help you discern what exactly needs to be done to place that necessary boundary between you and whatever is causing you harm, in order to bring that healing change in ways that only a boundary can.

cast it out

"Above all else, guard your heart, for everything you do flows from it."

Proverbs 4:23 NIV

Forgiveness

The simple definition of forgiveness is to stop feeling angry towards someone who has offended or hurt us in some way. But true forgiveness is not that simple, because forgiveness is a process that comes with many emotions to work through.

Feelings of betrayal, anger, bitterness, resentment, and heartache are just a few of the many emotions we may experience when someone has hurt or offended us. Issues of trust arise as well, when we now have doubts about the person who hurt us, and no assurance that they won't hurt us again. And finally, the questions come that totally throw us into forgiveness confusion; how can I excuse, condone, or forget the action they chose to do, that caused so much pain in my life?

The most important thing to remember about forgiveness is that its purpose is not for us to absolve a person from their mistake; that is between them and God. Our responsibility in forgiveness is to make that choice to let go of the offense that person bestowed upon us, to release the pain from the wound in our hearts, for if we let it remain there, it will eventually seethe into anger, resentment, and bitterness.

Forgiveness doesn't mean we have to forget, excuse, or be okay with what was done to us; we forgive so that the offense can no longer harm us or harden hearts. Anytime we carry any form of hatred in our hearts, we shut the door for love to come in, as well as flow out, for hatred and love cannot coexist in the same place together.

Forgiving someone doesn't give us a right to judge, condemn or convict another person, nor are we accountable to serve them justice for their actions. Forgiveness doesn't mean that we have to feel fondness for the person, or even like them, before we can forgive them. Forgiveness goes beyond all of these things, because forgiveness is for us to release our hearts to be healed, to be able to give and receive love once again.

Let's look at the two components of the word itself to better understand it's origin and definition: *for* and *give*. The word "for" means to move forward and to reach out for something, while the word "give" means to freely hand something over. Therefore, when we "for-give," we are choosing to willingly hand over all the negative feelings this offense has brought to us, so that we can move toward healing and cleansing our hearts to be renewed and become whole again.

God calls us to forgive one another so that our hearts can be pure to fully receive all the love that He has for us, as well as the love that comes from others.

When you have trouble releasing the harmful feelings that come from a hurt or offense that you have just walked through, ask God for His gift of the power to forgive, for He understands how difficult this can be for us, and He's always there to take our hand and walk us through the process of forgiveness.

Always remember that forgiveness is for you primarily; to release and restore all that was damaged, so that you can move on with peace in your heart once again.

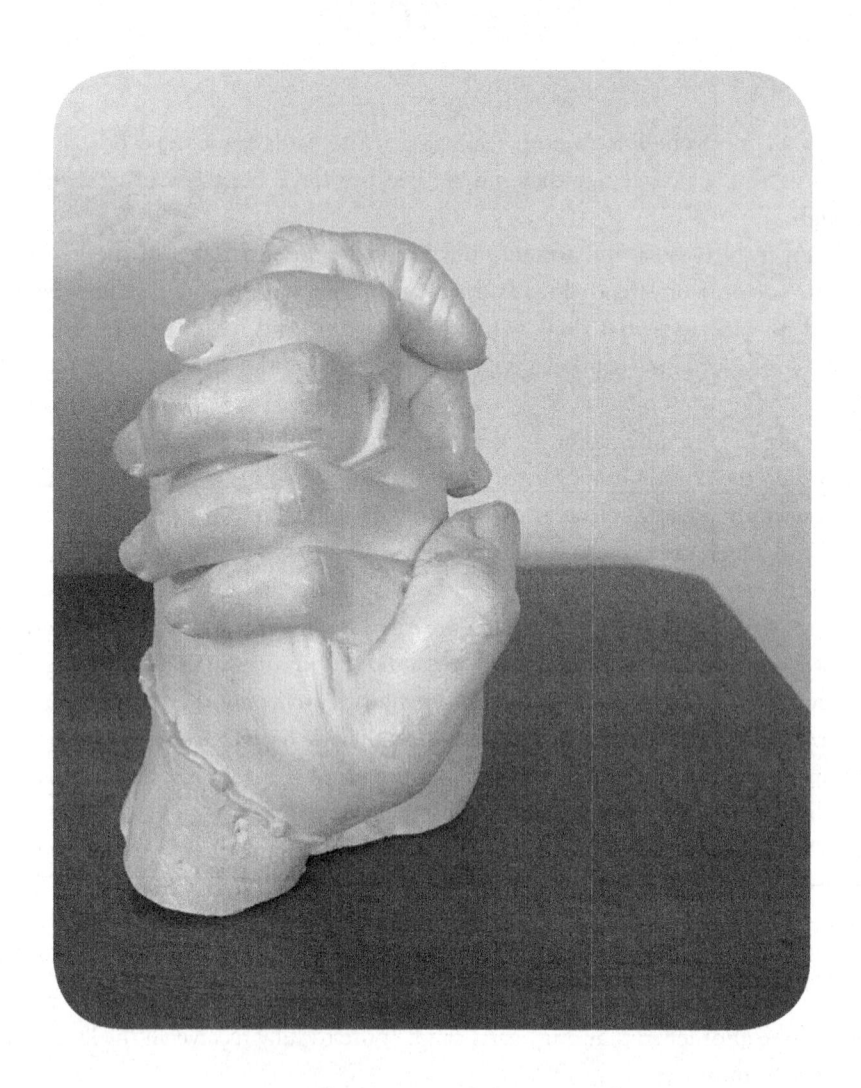

transfer more in a touch

"So he got up and went to his father. But while he was still a long way off, his father saw him and was filled with compassion for him; he ran to his son, threw his arms around him and kissed him."

Luke 15:20 NIV

Human Touch—The "Transferable" Sense

God created human beings with an incredible capacity to perceive and receive all we encounter. Our senses of sight, smell, hearing, taste, and touch allow us to experience life in a uniquely beautiful and physical way to be able to connect with each other and all that surrounds us in every way possible.

And although one sense is not more valuable than another, the sense of touch is exclusive in its ability to be transferred and shared in a more intimate way than any of the other senses can offer to us.

Touch is the very first sense we experience when we enter into this life from our mother's womb. We are "touched" by the careful hands that guide and assist our small, fragile bodies and welcome us into this sensory world to begin our life journey.

Science states that touch has the amazing ability to release calming endorphins, while reducing stress and nurturing a bond of trust and devotion. Think of when a baby cries; what comforts them more than anything? As we hold and embrace this tiny new life in our arms, our touch transfers love, security, and solace, as a feeling of peace begins to envelope them.

A sincere touch from one person to another will emit a feeling of greater closeness, comfort and understanding, by connecting our emotions in a deeper way, by physically transferring them through the unique sense of touch.

A loved one dies, a heart's been broken, a tragedy has left someone feeling devastated and lost, or one has suffered a great disappointment from a dream that has gone amiss; are just a few of life's circumstances that require more than only spoken words or an ear to listen can offer. These life situations require an extra special kind of comfort, that can only be fulfilled by a loving human touch.

A hug to offer a deeper sense of sympathy when words just aren't enough, a gentle hand laid upon the shoulder of another for reassurance, or a connection of two hands intertwined to let someone know that you're right there beside them, to offer love, sympathy, and support in ways that nothing else can.

Each of our senses are precious, but as we age and grow older, many of them tend to lose some of their vitality and resilience except for our sense of touch, which is able to maintain its dynamic power in spirit, from the first day of our journey all the way through to the last. No matter how strong we are or weak we become, a touch will never diminish in it's beautiful purpose and the amazing effect it will always be able to have in another person's life.

Never ignore or lose sight of the amazing ability and purpose that only the sense of touch has to offer; connecting those innermost places within each of us with one another to bring God's love even closer to us.

celebrate transformations

"See, I am doing a new thing! Now it springs up; do you not perceive it?
I am making a way in the wilderness and streams in the wasteland."

Isaiah 43:19 NIV

A Wedding Is More Than

When my daughter Sarah brought us the news that she was engaged, our lives became consumed with planning a beautiful wedding for her. Excitement took hold and the journey began to reach that destination of the perfect wedding day. A wedding, a birth, a new home, a new career, and so many other wonderful life transitions that we travel through always bring "more than" we realize or expect, as we prepare for these life changing moments.

We were blessed in every way on that day; God gave us the gift of a celebration that went well beyond our own expectations, with extra special blessings and memories to cherish for the rest of our lives. A few days later, as I sat in a quiet moment to reflect on all that the last year had brought, I realized that a wedding (or any significant life changing celebration) brings so much more than a day of celebration.

It is a journey beyond the planning, the traditions, the dresses, cake, and flowers, becoming a voyage of perseverance, patience, perspectives, emotions, and character. It brings out the good, the bad, the beautiful, and yes, the ugly at times, of each person. Each individual with their own thoughts, ideas and dreams, coming together to plan a "perfect" day, while knowing that nothing is ever "perfect" makes the whole process quite a challenge and very interesting at times!

Words are spoken out of places filled with too much worry, tears flow from eyes that are overwhelmed and tired, nerves sizzle with each new detail that comes out of nowhere. Wedding dementia takes hold, disrupting the normal routines of life, and people become someone else, in the craziness of it all!

With that being said, as we step out of the madness, there are so many things that are changing and becoming new, beyond the "wedding," beyond whatever it is we are celebrating that is creating a new future for everyone.

A daughter is starting a new life, a family is growing into more, a mom and dad are letting go. Every life is changing and transforming into something new and different. Each person has their own feelings and what this all means to them, facing individual changes, all different from each other's.

And through all of this, relationships are made, foundations are born, and we all come together in new ways for this beautiful life transition that is taking place. We learn new things about each other as well as ourselves and come to a greater understanding of the things that truly matter. We learn what love, compassion and patience are when we choose to take our "selves" out of the picture and see what is actually happening all around us.

The "perfect" plan will have its glitches and unexpected challenges, for no plan is ever the same "perfect" in each individual's eyes, yet it will be these exact imperfect moments that will bring us new doors of opportunity to learn, grow and become even closer as we move beyond the beautiful celebration that is now just a cherished memory into the new journey ahead and all it has waiting to offer to each of us.

A wedding IS SO MUCH MORE! I am so grateful for all that has come and look forward to the future of so much more.

seeds of promise

"All you need to say is simply 'yes' or 'no'; anything beyond this comes from the evil one."

Matthew 5:37 NIV

Honor Your Promises

Our words convey a lot about us, especially when we make commitments and promises to one another. Yet our words alone hold no purpose or meaning at all, if we don't back them up with the actions to fulfill our intentions.

It's easy to say aloud our well-meaning intentions; we want to help, volunteer, meet with a friend, join a group, and on and on, without thinking about how someone else's life will be affected when we choose to not honor the words that were spoken.

When we say "Yes, I will," or "Let's do this," we are making a commitment to someone else to carry out what we said we would do. Words spoken with affirmative intentions need to be fulfilled with the actions it takes to complete the promise. Commitments are not meant to be just wishful intentions to be taken lightly or completely forgotten; they are a vow that comes with an assurance of trust for the person who is relying and depending on us.

I think we need to take a step back and be more aware of how a promise that is left unfulfilled can truly affect the life of another. That offer to have coffee, call, or stop by may be the only thing someone has to look forward to that week. That committee you volunteered for will now have to work harder until they find someone else to take your place when you decide "not" to show up to fulfill the pledge you made. Commitments left unfulfilled not only disappoint but can truly hurt others in more ways than we realize.

Before you speak, before you promise, before you commit to anything at all, just remember that your words are being heard by another, and that person is depending on you to keep your promise for reasons that truly matter to them.

We all have good intentions in those moments when we promise something to others, but if you find yourself thinking maybe, I might, I'm not quite sure, then just say no or nothing at all, and if you can't fulfill a promise you made for some reason, at least let them know so they aren't left in a difficult place.

Our promises impact the lives of others as well as ourselves, and we need to put honor behind each promise we make, for God calls us to be accountable in all we do and say.

moving forward

"The Lord is close to the brokenhearted and saves those who are crushed in Spirit."

Psalm 34:18 NIV

Traveling Through Life's Losses

The most difficult paths we travel through in life are those of loss. Loss of a loved one, the end of a relationship, losing a job that's been part of your life purpose can all leave us feeling lost within ourselves and in our lives.

Each loss changes everything, including ourselves, for what we knew as secure and safe is no longer and our lives are dramatically changed in so many ways forever.

Fear and confusion creep into every crevice of our being, and we now have to face all those vulnerable emotions that emerge, those feelings we have never had before and have no idea what to do with now.

When I lost my Dad, I lost my sense of security; he was my rock and I could depend on him for almost everything. Losing my two children left me with the saddest of realities: that I would never be able to bear another child and be a mom again. When I lost my Mom, I lost my best friend and all the losses that come with that.

Loss leaves us broken, confused, and hurting, with many hallways of grief to walk through while we continue to try to go on with our lives and find our new normal, even though nothing feels like it will ever be right again.

The most important thing to remember during any great loss in our lives is that we must grieve what we've lost in order to heal and find closure, to be able to move on with the rest of our lives and not stay lost in the sadness.

Grief is personal to each of us and does not work the same for everyone; the time, the steps, and the healing will vary from person to person. However, if you find yourself drowning in feelings of hopelessness, sorrow, and despair, to the point you can no longer function in daily life, you may be stuck in the stage of depression: the hallway of grief that is the longest to walk through and will keep you from any kind of healing and closure.

And though you may have great faith and trust, you may find that you need some outside help and should never feel guilty about that. God understands how difficult this process is, and while he comforts you during this time of mourning, He will also bring others to love, encourage, and support you as you go through this grueling journey.

No one can get through grief alone, and that's why there are so many resources available to help with the grieving process. Don't be ashamed or feel like you're weak, if you need to reach out for that extra help.

Find someone you can share your feelings with: a trusted friend, a spiritual leader, a counselor, or support group are all wonderful resources that can help you with the grief you are going through.

Life does go on after loss and although things will now be different forever, you will find a way to be happy once again, once you heal from your loss and keep moving forward so you can live out the rest of your life in the best way possible.

keep on keeping on

"...being strengthened with all power according to his glorious might
so that you may have great endurance and patience...."

Collisions 1:11 NIV

Strength to Persevere

Perseverance is a choice in commitment to keep on keeping on no matter what obstacles life places along our paths.

Perseverance takes stamina, patience, and a strength to endure, along with faith and trust to see that the road we are traveling is worth every effort, while being able to see light at the end of every dark tunnel we're walking through, no matter how overwhelming it seems to us.

One of the greatest examples in my life of true endurance and perseverance was my Mom. She grew up in an orphanage during her early childhood years, followed by a foster home, until she turned eighteen and then went to live with a friend and her family. She had no true family connections; her life depended completely on her, and even though she endured such a difficult and challenging beginning, she never quit, gave up, or felt sorry for herself. She truly was a pioneer of sorts, given the times she lived in back then: a woman supporting herself when most women were not.

She married my Dad and went on to raise a family of four children, working very hard to be a good wife and mother, which I have to believe was more challenging for her than for most of us, since she had never had a family foundation to give her any type of guidance as to how to even be a wife, mom, and to nurture a family. Her spirit to persevere is the greatest model of commitment that I have ever seen, and this is the beautiful inheritance that she left with me; the piece of her that continues to live on in me and is always my inspiration to never quit or give up, and to always keep on going.

My Mom's determination was not only from her strong will to survive, it came from that deep place of faith she held in her heart. Christ's strength that lived within her and His love that protected, provided, and guided her were what kept her safe and gave her the ability to keep pushing through a life that was full of many hard knocks.

When we make the choice to keep on going, to keep on trusting, and to keep on believing in Him, God gives us the power to get through the seemingly impossible places we find ourselves in. The strength that comes from the Spirit that dwells within each of us, is what enables us to push against the forces of life that try to disable us and gives us all we need to persevere in the most trying of circumstances.

Life here on earth will always have its troubles, obstacles, and challenges to work through, but as long as we pull Christ's strength from within us, we will be able to persevere through all things to continue this beautiful journey set before us.

quiet contemplation

"Let the Spirit change your way of thinking."

Ephesians 4:23 CEV

Change Begins with Just One Thought

The first step to change begins with the way we think. Our thoughts control us, drive us, and sometimes even hurt us, depending on how we choose to perceive what surrounds us and how we choose to *think about it*. Our thoughts are uniquely ours, and although no one else think "for" us, the world and others can certainly influence our individual thought process. Thoughts are the impressions we place upon our minds that generate every decision we make and direct the course our lives will take. Our thoughts connect to the emotions we hold in our hearts and will also determine how we feel about life.

God created us with this wonderful ability to think on our own, giving us the free will to *choose* our own thoughts. Our perspectives, decisions, and even our characters are created by what we think about, so if you want to change anything at all in your life, you need to transform and renew what you're thinking about. It truly is that easy and, yet it is not, because thoughts become so ingrained in us, and to think any other way can actually frighten us. When we change our thoughts we change our lives, and even positive changes can become quite overwhelming.

One thought ignites another, each one building upon the other, so when we change just that one thought, we can change our entire way of thinking. Let's say you have a goal to get healthy. Do you tell yourself you *want* to get healthy and then do nothing, or do you ask yourself *how* can I get healthier and look for ways that will help you get there? Affirmative thoughts, such as I can and I will, open doors of opportunity to the changes we are looking for, while negative thoughts, such as I can't or I don't know how, just set us up for failure before we even have a chance to begin.

God tells us to lean on His understanding and that means that we need to be open to His way of thinking. He will help us through any thought transformation we are facing, when we come to Him and ask for His wisdom and help while being willing to let go of our own way of thinking and open ourselves up to receive His renewed thoughts for us.

When I find myself stuck in a place that needs change, I know I must first choose to let go of the thoughts that imprison me to make room for the new way of thinking that God is bringing to me.

Give your troubling thoughts to God and allow Him to give you a *mind makeover*, as He leads you on a new and straight path to change the thoughts that have been holding you back.

God's perfect timing

"He has made everything beautiful in its time. He has also set eternity in the human heart; yet no one can fathom what God has done from beginning to end."

Ecclesiastes 3:11 NIV

Give God Time

We may not think that God needs our patience, but He does. You may be thinking "but God is God;" He can do all things and time is not an obstacle for Him. And though this is true, while He is working "for" us, He is also working "through" us, and many times "within" us.

God gives us this wonderful gift called free will, the ability and the opportunity to make our own decisions. Our choices not only impact ourselves, they influence the lives of others in more ways than we realize. Choices affect one choice to another, and as God works on an answer for us, He too has to wait on all of the choices of others.

God is a gentleman and doesn't "force" His way into our lives; He lets us decide if we want to walk with Him or if we do not. And this is exactly why He needs us to be patient with Him, just as He has to wait patiently on us as we make our own decisions.

God works behind the scenes for us all the time and has a lot of details to arrange and coordinate for any plan to materialize. God may call someone to something He desires to use them for, and depending on whether that person says yes or no will determine if He has to change His whole plan— and that may take Him a little more time.

The wonderful thing about God is that His plans consider every detail and obstacle, and He needs time to make all these things work out before He gives us the best answer possible.

So, when you think about all the things that God must wait for, you can understand why we need to be patient with Him. When we learn to be patient with Him, we also receive an additional gift, and that is the opportunity to grow stronger in our faith and trust. As God waits on us and we wait on Him, we can nurture a closer relationship with each other.

God wants to answer our prayers as quickly as possible, and while He works on one prayer, He is also working simultaneously on the prayers of others. Our individual prayers open doors for Him to not only bring what we need, but to also address the needs of others, as he works His good through each of us and will always bring the best answer to every prayer.

Have patience with God and while you wait, rest in the joy of knowing that He is working out all we cannot, to give each of us even more than what we originally asked for.

keep an eye out

"Who can hide in secret places so that I cannot see them?" declares the Lord.
"Do not I fill heaven and earth?" declares the Lord.

Jeremiah 23:24 NIV

God is Everywhere When We Look for Him

In order to see God in our lives we have to look for Him. Yes, He is always with and amongst us, but when we take God's presence for granted and don't focus on how He interacts with us, we won't be able to see much of Him.

The thing to remember is this; God is connected to each of us in such a personal and intricate way, and only He knows exactly what we each need to "see" in order to find Him; we just have to open our eyes, ears and hearts to find Him in these places.

God is everywhere and has so many ways that He shows himself to us, but if we aren't looking for Him, we may miss Him completely.

God gives us signs all of the time and "speaks" to us in many different ways. That small voice in your subconscious that keeps nudging you with a thought or idea, that person He places in your day that says just what you needed to hear, or that message or quote you see that totally speaks to your heart are just some of the ways that God speaks with us.

We can find His wisdom, comfort, guidance, and truth when we open our eyes to all that surrounds us and look for Him in everything.

When my Mom passed away, I asked for a sign that she was at peace, and God sent me a butterfly. I asked for a dream to have one last conversation with my Dad after he passed, and God gave me not one, but two dream dialogues with him. When I'm lonely, He always sends a friend, and when I'm lost and confused He brings his words of encouragement through my journaling and daily inspirational reading.

God sends us gentle reminders of His presence in our daily lives as well, through our normal everyday activities. You remember something you almost forgot, you find something you've lost, or something appears of out of nowhere that makes you smile when you're feeling down.

God's presence is always active, alive and well in our lives, and all we have to do to see more of Him is to look for Him in all things!

light of truth

"I have no greater joy than to hear that my children are walking in the truth."

3 John 1:4 NIV

The Truth About Truth

Truth is defined as something that is factual, concrete, and indisputable, such as black is black, time always moves on, and the earth revolves around the sun.

Yet when it comes to our individual truth, the facts may not be as clear, for what holds true for one person can be quite different for someone else.

Each person's truth comes from a personal and vulnerable place, because we are all unique and different from one another. Our truths define who we are based on our own life experiences. Our foundation of truth comes from the beliefs we were taught, the morals and values instilled within us, and how we choose to perceive what truth really means to us.

Sometimes truth gets buried beneath our fears, our pain, and the anger or bitterness we carry deep inside of our hearts. If we truly want to seek out truth in our lives, we must go to a very delicate place within and be humbly honest with ourselves.

You've heard the saying "the truth hurts," as well as "the truth will set you free," and both of these statements are true in their own specific ways. It can be quite painful to face the truth head on at first, but once you let go of those secrets you've been hiding behind, your heart will be liberated from that weight you've been carrying around for so long.

One of the greatest truths I have ever faced in my own life was seeing that there was a very selfish side to me. I was, am and always will be that person with a heart to give and to be there for anyone in need. But what I failed to see for many years was that my giving came with a personal expectation to always receive something in return. Whether it be a compliment, a thank you, a reciprocal gesture, or even a feeling, my heart was not selfless enough to give at its full potential. It wasn't until I humbly admitted this truth to myself that God could finally change and renew this part of me.

Jesus tells us He is the way, the truth, and the life, and for us to allow His truth to shine through us, we must first face the truth within ourselves. His truth brings the strength and clarity we need to accept and acknowledge those truths that we've buried, while His grace guides and comforts us as we go through the process.

The truth is the only way to emerge from those dark places that lurk deep within, because truth is the light that illuminates who we truly are and will always be good to us.

When you are troubled and seeking to find that truth that will release you to live without guilt and condemnation any longer, look up to receive your truth through Jesus and set your heart free once again.

unique & beautiful

"I praise you because I am fearfully and wonderfully made;
your works are wonderful, I know that full well."

Psalm 139:14 NIV

Don't Let Others Edit Your Definition

God wrote a unique definition for each of us, so why do we care so much about what others think of us and allow their perceptions to define who we are?

To be loved is one of our greatest human needs, and we want everyone to "like" us; however, we need to remember that love is not earned, it is freely given.

We are all beautifully different, because God knew exactly what He was doing when He created each one of us. Our gifts, our personalities, and even our appearances are individual and unique to only us, and we each play a special role in His divine plan. Yet so many times, we are willing to change and compromise who we are for the sake of others, to gain their love, respect, and acceptance.

We are not here to re-create the person God created in order to please everyone else; we are here to serve God and fulfill His will by being exactly who we are. Anytime we feel the need to change or compromise for another person, we need to reevaluate that relationship, before we lose our true identity.

I spent many years of my life believing that I had to be the "someone" that other people expected me to be "for" them. If I didn't act, react, or even feel the way that they thought I should, they would judge me, reject me, and no longer like me.

I thought I had to prove myself worthy to be loved by anyone, and I became very lost and depressed and realized that by trying to be someone other than who I truly was left me feeling lonelier and more rejected than ever.

I lost my true "me" for many years, until I finally understood that if others can't accept you for who you are, flaws and all, then maybe that someone isn't a part of God's plan for your life in the way that you thought.

Those who see you only through their eyes of self-centered needs and what makes them comfortable will never be able to see your true definition, and no amount of effort you make will ever be able to change that.

God brings those into our lives who will love, support, and accept us for who we are, so we need to stop trying to change for those who do not.

Keep your eyes on the "you" that God created, that person whom He loves like crazy, and never allow the perception or opinion of others to change the wonderful definition that God has already given to you. We choose how we let others treat us, so make your own choice to be around only those who love you first and foremost for the beautiful person that God created in you.

gentle pruning

"He cuts off every branch in me that bears no fruit, while every branch that does bear fruit he prunes so that it will be even more fruitful."

John 15:2 NIV

God is Our Gardener

The bible tells us that God cuts away every branch that does not bear fruit in us. For many years I didn't quite understand the full message of this scripture because I couldn't get past wondering why God would cut anything away from me. It seemed like such a painful process and one I was certainly not wanting to experience. To me it meant that I must be so flawed and unpleasing in God's eyes for Him to sever off parts of me, and then I wondered what would be left and who would I be.

Thankfully today, I have come to understand the true meaning of this wonderful scripture, and now look at it as one of the most loving things He does for us. God never takes anything away without replacing it with something better, and this comes through God's gentle pruning process.

I have a beautiful hydrangea bush in my garden. Every early Spring, I gently cut off the dead branches from the previous year to give it new wood to grow and thrive on. The times I've neglected to prune this plant, it didn't flourish well at all, because the old dead branches could no longer nurture new flowers.

God does this same thing for us, in ways that only He can, by lovingly trimming away those dead branches that inhibit new growth in us. He is the vine, the foundation of our being, and His life cannot reach us through any place of dormancy or deadness.

God has many ways in which He prunes us; some may be more painful than we would prefer, but when we see the beautiful growth that emerges, we will thank Him for the tender Hands that He placed upon us during the pruning process.

He changes our hearts by bringing new thoughts of insight and understanding, he teaches us wonderful lessons from all that we walk through to strengthen and grow us and helps us to let go of all that no longer brings good to our lives. As He gently trims away those branches that are no longer useful to us, His vine of foundation is renewed within us, and all that was good before can now take root even more, to become more fruitful and beautiful.

Pruning rejuvenates, renews, and restores us. Nothing can grow from something that's dead; change cannot come from stagnant places, and life's seasons need pruning to keep us alive and thriving.

When God's pruning shears come your way, relax and submit to His loving hands, knowing that as He is gently trimming away, He is preparing something new and wonderful to grow within you.

hear the "whispers"

"And he who searches our hearts knows the mind of the Spirit,
because the Spirit intercedes for God's people in accordance with the will of God."

Romans 8:27 NIV

The Spirit Makes All the Difference

When we accept Jesus as our Lord and Savior, we acknowledge that He died for our sins to save us and are promised eternal life in Heaven. This is the beginning of our journey in Faith, but there is so much more beyond this first step, when we choose to invite the Holy Spirit to come live within us.

When we live in the Spirit we become connected with God on a whole new level. We see more of Him in everything, hear his voice in the deepest places within our hearts, and feel his presence in ways we've never felt before. The Spirit is our guide in all things as we travel our journey here on earth.

Through the Spirit we are renewed, become one with God and begin a true personal relationship with Him to receive all He has for us, and be all we are for Him. God is the Spirit and the Spirit is God, and though they are one, they are each their own and unique in what they bring to us.

The Holy Spirit is our prayer partner and intercedes for us when our hearts cannot express in words what we need God to hear; He is the line of communication between us and God.

The Holy Spirit changes any unpleasing desires we may have and aligns them with God's will for us. He helps us see truth through God's eyes and changes our hearts in the places we cannot.

We receive His Fruit, the gifts of love, joy, peace, patience, kindness, goodness, faithfulness, gentleness, and self-control. These wonderful gifts change everything, as they fill our hearts with the same kind of love that God has for us: a love founded in faithfulness, commitment, and good will, that now shines from within us to spread God's light.

The Holy Spirit is the breath of God within us, the life partner whom Jesus left with us after He ascended into heaven, whom brings "life" into our lives in a way that nothing or no one else can.

When we choose to live in the Spirit, we are protected from the ways of the world that can bring harm and turmoil to our souls and distance us from our Father. The Spirit keeps us grounded, humble, stable, and pure, while giving us the peace and joy to truly live an abundant life in every way.

The Holy Spirit is available to each of us; however, He is a gentleman who will never force His way into any heart, and, therefore, it is up to us to invite Him into our lives. Welcome the Holy Spirit into your heart today and you will be amazed at what a difference His presence will make, as you are renewed to receive all of the wonderful things that the Spirit is waiting to bring to your life.

wall of divide

"Accept one another, then just as Christ accepted you,
in order to bring praise to God."

Romans 15:7 NIV

Rejection and Judgement

Rejection hurts, no questions asked. Anytime we are dismissed by others, it doesn't feel good! Yet, people reject each other in ways they may not even see, and I think we really need to think about how certain actions can be taken as rejection.

When we say no to someone with no explanation, we are saying that we don't care about their feelings or thoughts in a situation. When we ignore others completely, we are conveying to them that they hold no importance in our lives and are not worthy of our time, according to us.

That text or voicemail you chose not to answer, that plan you made and never followed through on or didn't show up for, or even when you don't give someone your full attention while they are talking to you; are some of the many ways that we reject one other.

Anytime we put our own interests first, with no respect or care as to how our choices will affect someone else, we are judging them according to the standards that we have set, as to whether or not they are important enough to be acknowledged or included in our life. These choices are degrading and humiliating to a person's self-worth and are one of the most harmful things we can do to one another.

There are two things in life that hurt me more than anything else: one is to be unjustly judged, and the other is to be ignored. What I've come to understand about these two things is that many times one is the cause of the other.

When we choose to judge, we base our choice to ignore or reject someone on only our own thoughts and opinions of them, and when we choose to dismiss someone for any reason, it most likely began with a judgement we had already formed about them.

Judging or ignoring anyone makes that person feel like they are unloved, forgotten, and that they don't really matter, and each one of those feelings hurts just as much as the other.

God put us all here together to respect, support and acknowledge each other, never to reject, ignore, or cast anyone out for any reason. One of his greatest commandments is to love one another, and to judge and dismiss someone holds no love at all.

Jesus was rejected numerous times during His time here on earth, and the Bible tells us how painful that was for Him. If rejection hurt the Son of God, why would we believe it would hurt us any less.

We need to be more self-aware in all of the choices we make that impact the lives of others, especially when it comes to ignoring or leaving someone out, because no one deserves to be judged and rejected by anyone.

balance

"Truly he is my rock and my salvation;
he is my fortress, I will never be shaken."

Psalm 62:2 NIV

God is Our Balance

When life gets tough and overwhelming, sometimes our faith can waver. We get so caught up in all that's happening around us and forget that we have a partner to keep us stable, who can conquer any struggle, battle, or life change that we are facing, and that partner's name is God.

When we trust God in everything, He'll never allow us to lean too far over before He comes rushing in to lift us up with His loving hands and keeps us from falling off the ledge we are teetering on. God is our center, our strong foundation, who keeps our lives level when we face those things that attempt to push us off balance.

When we are sad He brings comfort, and walks us through these dark places. He wraps His arms of love around us in a continual hug, to let us know that He is there for us.

If we are confused, He brings us His wisdom and knowledge so that we can find His answer in what we are seeking.

The times that fear creeps into our hearts, we can run to Him for safety, knowing He is always protecting us in ways that only He can.

When we get lost on those dark paths that sometimes come before us, God shines His light even brighter and guides us out of the shadows.

He brings us truth when we are vulnerable to Satan's lies, He draws closer to us when we are lonely, and He puts out the fire of anger within our hearts when we find ourselves faced with these troubling emotions, by bringing His peace and understanding.

Whenever I feel I'm falling too far in the wrong direction, I reach out to God and hold on even tighter in Faith and trust, knowing He will never let me fall over any farther.

Nothing we face in life is too difficult for God because He prevails over all things, and we can find our footing once again, when we place our trust in Him.

Anytime you feel your world shaking, you can lean on God and His strength will hold you up until you find your footing once again.

I know that was you, God!

"For it is by grace you have been saved, through faith;
and this is not from yourselves, it is the gift of God."

Ephesians 2:8 NIV

His Amazing Grace is Our Daily Miracle

Miracles are defined as improbable or extraordinary life events that bring very welcome outcomes: those times that God brings those extra special blessings that leave us in awe of what just happened.

An illness with a hopeless diagnosis is healed, that new job you interviewed for and haven't heard back from for so long is suddenly offered to you, you're in a terrible accident that should have left you greatly harmed, but yet you emerge with not even a scratch, or that money you so desperately need for something is provided at just the right moment — these are what we commonly define as miracles.

I have been blessed with many extraordinary miracles in my life: a broken marriage four days away from signing divorce papers fully restored by God's hand of Grace, a clean biopsy, a huge debt relieved beyond anything I could have done on my own, and jobs that came when just about all hope had been lost.

Those times in our lives when all seems impossible and hopeless, when God blesses us with more than anything we "thought" could ever be possible, are the things we clearly see as extraordinary miracles.

But there are also the everyday miracles as well, the ones that may seem more ordinary and not so extraordinary to us. Our health, our family, our home, and all our needs provided for are God's exceptional gifts we receive every day, but don't always give as much notice to. We tend to take these things more for granted, rather than seeing them as the tremendous blessings they truly are.

The strength, discipline, and determination to do all we need in a day, when we feel we have nothing left to give, come from the miracle of His amazing Grace.

The healing that comes after loss with new hope to go on, the comfort from a friend when we're feeling down and out, answers to daily prayers for patience and understanding in the most gruelling of situations, as well as the blanket of protection continually placed over us—these are what we may see as "ordinary," yet are no less "extraordinary" than those that are more noticeably spectacular.

Life is our daily miracle, as each new day begins with God's renewed grace and mercy, and no matter what yesterday brought or left behind, we receive endless second chances to renew and refresh our lives as He continually opens the doors that will lead to all of the new miracles He is preparing for us.

Nothing in life is ordinary, and when we open our eyes to see each day as the amazing gift it truly is, we become more aware of how miraculously blessed we are with more than we deserve, and more than we could ever do on our own!

And this is called God's amazing Grace, the most extraordinary miracle of all!

just say no

"Do not make friends with a hot-tempered person, do not associate with one easily angered, or you may learn their ways and get yourself ensnared."

Proverbs 22:24-29 NIV

Misery's Invitation

There is an old saying that "misery loves company," and this statement holds more truth than we may recognize or pay much notice to.

When people are sad, distressed, or angry, the last thing they want is to see others happy. It's not because they wish bad things on others; they just don't want to feel miserable alone.

In many ways, they are actually seeking comfort, understanding, and sympathy, but instead of vulnerably admitting this and reaching out, they believe that sharing their misery will somehow make them feel better.

The emotions they feel are so overwhelming, and the reasons behind these emotions come from a place of fear, due to the deeper issues they aren't ready or able to face. Misery is a mask we hide behind when we don't like what the mirror in front of is trying to show us.

Misery feeds on itself, and when we join into its company with anyone, we are only adding fuel to an already raging fire, while allowing it to spread farther and wider.

So how do we help those who are attempting to get us to join in their company of misery, while protecting ourselves from those projected arrows of their suffering that they are aiming at us?

The most important thing I think we can do when we see someone struggling in these distressful situations is take them aside and show them we care, by offering to have a compassionate conversation with them. A conversation to truly listen to their feelings, with no judgement, opinions, or even advice.

When we join them in this way, we open that door for them to feel safe in those vulnerable places, to help them work through whatever is causing them to be so miserable, as we pray that they see God's light shining through us, from His Spirit within us.

However, if a person wants to continue to stay miserable and has no desire to receive help or support, wanting nothing more than companionship in this desolate place they choose to remain in, we must know when it's time to move away from that invitation before it brings damage to our own lives.

It can be so tempting and very easy to jump into the problems of others, especially when we truly care about them. We may even think that we are giving them support in this way, but when we engage in anyone else's projected displeasure, we are only bringing more harm to both them and ourselves.

Whenever we encounter those who are trying to invite us into these indignant places, we must ask God for discernment, to be able to know whether they are truly reaching out for help, or only looking for company to be miserable with them.

Misery loves company for so many different reasons, and we must always be aware of each individual objective that accompanies it, and never get caught up in someone else's misery for all the wrong motivations that will allow that same kind of distress to enter into our lives as well.

His delicate touch

"Create in me a new heart, O God, and renew a steadfast spirit within me."

Psalm 51:10 NIV

Only God Can Truly Change a Troubled Heart

God creates each of us with a pure and loving heart, and as we travel along our life journey, our hearts can take a detour from that perfect beginning and change in ways that no longer come from that beautiful place.

When our hearts become tainted with anger, bitterness, resentment and hatred, those emotions that hold us prisoner and are resistant to any change we alone can make, it's time to call on God to bring us a change of heart.

God can change any heart that needs a makeover in ways that only He can. He can bring peace and forgiveness to a heart that struggles, soften a heart that's taken on hardness, and remove that selfish part within that has taken over our love and compassion for others.

God knows our hearts better than we do ourselves and can reach into those places that we alone cannot. He knows exactly how to align our thoughts, desires, perspectives, and anything else that's necessary, to bring that significant change to a heart that has become lost within itself.

Only God can turn hate into love, selfishness into giving, and pride into humility, because only God can bring true and lasting change to our hearts, through His unconditional love for us.

The key to any heart transformation is to let Him "in" and allow Him to work "on" us. We have to let go of our own control and open ourselves up to His will for us.

It's a choice we make, for God is gentle and won't ever "force" His way into our hearts, but He is always there waiting for us to ask for His help and will bring all we need to renew and restore any part of our heart that is damaged or stuck in a difficult place.

Our hearts go through a lot during our lifetimes, and the changes that come are inevitable, but as long as we call on God when we feel our hearts headed in the wrong direction, we'll always be protected from the outside sources that are trying to change our hearts in a negative way, because God lives in each of us and is the best heart changer there is.

Give your troubled heart to Him and watch Him work His amazing in you, as He not only changes your heart, but changes your life in ways that are only possible through Him.

a place to gather

"As Jesus and his disciples were on their way, he came to a village where a woman named Martha opened her home to him."

Luke 10:38 NIV

Spend "Real" Time Together

One of my favorite things to do is to gather with friends and family at each other's homes, to spend what I like to call "real time" together.

Life is so busy these days, and though we meet for many reasons in many different places, it ends up being more about the particular commitment or obligation we are attending, rather than to just spend true time together with one another.

It seems like we've fallen into the practice that we need a specific outside occasion, excuse, or venue of entertainment to meet with each other and have become more resistant to inviting others into our homes just to spend time together.

We go to concerts, sporting events, movies, and things that we share similar interests in, to make these experiences even more enjoyable and fulfilling. Although these are all wonderful things to do together, they don't bring the same kind of intimate connection as when we spend time at our homes with one another for no other purpose than "being" together.

Home truly is where the heart lives; our personal sanctuary where we can feel comfortable just being ourselves and welcome others in to do just the same. At home we are more relaxed, less distracted, and can truly focus on those whom we love and cherish.

Home is that safe place where we can have those meaningful and honest conversations, without worrying about how loud we talk, laugh, or cry if we need to. Home is the place we can sit around the dinner table for hours, have casual Summer cookouts on our patios, or gather around a fire to catch up on our lives, while enjoying each other's company and nurturing true bonded relationships.

The Bible has many stories that tell us how Jesus gathered with others to share a meal and have good conversation. The first churches began in people's homes, before there were temples and big fancy buildings, as people gathered in the dwellings of one another to worship and study God's word.

Home is where everything begins and ends each day of our lives; it's the place we always come back to, and to share this blessing with others, unites us in a special way like nothing else can.

When we open our homes up to one another, we open our hearts to each other, to create the best memories and relationships that will last forever, as we spend "real" time together.

faith

"You see that his faith and actions were working together,
and his faith was made complete by what he did."

James 2:22 NIV

Activate Your Faith

Faith is the gift we receive when we make the choice to place our belief and trust in God. We are confident in His existence, we trust in His word, and we feel His amazing presence in our lives.

But Faith isn't only a gift to be left buried within our hearts and kept to ourselves, Faith is a call to action in our choice to follow God. When we use this gift as our foundation to lead and guide us in every direction, we bring this gift of Faith to life!

God tells us in James 2:17 that faith by itself, if not accompanied by works, is dead. In 2Corinthians 5:7 He says, we are to walk by faith, not by sight. Notice that both of these statements are calling us to "use" this gift by taking some kind of action.

Faith begins as a seed that needs to be watered and nurtured in order to grow into something more wonderful.

We can believe in many things; a dream, a goal, a change we need to make, but if we only see these things as a possibility, and take no action to set them in motion, sooner or later we'll lose these ambitions and they will never amount to anything.

This same concept holds true in our Faith, for if we don't move in our Faith, it will only remain a tiny seed that will never have the opportunity to break out of its shell, to become all that it was created for.

Through Faith we receive the direction, wisdom, and clarity to find our true purpose in His will for us. It's the gift that keeps giving and growing, because the more Faithful we are, the more Faith we receive from Him.

Faith holds us accountable in our actions, thoughts, and even walks us through our emotions, when we choose to put God first in everything.

Faith is like our personal life instruction manual that teaches us how to treat others, gets us through all of our struggles, and gives us something greater to trust in, believe, and follow, when life gets confusing and overwhelming.

When we get our direction from Him and hear and obey all He tells us to do, our Faith becomes active as His light shines through us onto all those who cross our paths. Our actions set the examples for others to see more of God in their lives and gives them the opportunity to make the same choice as we have; to believe and receive this amazing gift He offers to each of us.

Our faith is the assurance of God's presence within our lives, our trust is the choice to follow His path, and our actions allow Him to work through us, so we no longer only "believe" He exists, but we also actively follow God's plans to bring Him to life here on our earthly journey.

apprehension

"Rejoice always, pray continually, give thanks in all circumstances;
for this is God's will for you in Christ."

1Thessalonians 5:16-18 NIV

Puddles of Dread

Life can become more dreadful than joyful, when all of the commitments and responsibilities we are held to leave us feeling like we're constantly trudging through puddles of mud to get these things done.

Cleaning the house, doing the laundry, grocery shopping and meal planning aren't always what we look forward to, but yet need to be done—over and over.

We dread the thought of doing these things, we resent the time it takes to do them, and we don't enjoy the process as we walk through them.

Sadly, we become so accustomed to this mindset of dread, that we don't even realize what this attitude and perspective is taking away from our lives.

Dread robs us of seeing the blessings, opportunities, and all of the good that God brings through all we do. All of those things that we don't look forward to have a greater meaning in our lives, which we will only be able to see and receive if we choose to readjust our outlook and way of thinking.

I think the best way to resist dread in our lives is to take on an attitude of gratitude. That house you have to clean, is the home God provides to keep you warm, safe and protected. The grocery shopping puts food on the table to ensure you will be fed and well nourished, and the laundry signifies that you have clothes to wear on your back. The bills you need to pay are a great reminder that you have all the things you need and more to live life comfortably.

We can turn our dread into joy when we change the way we look at things and find ways to make these dreaded chores more enjoyable. While you clean, you can pray or listen to music to make the task more pleasant. While you are grocery shopping, be more aware of those who God may place along your path to offer a smile or hello to. When paying the bills, thank God for the provision for every check that you write.

Like that puddle of mud you see up ahead, you can either choose to walk through it and end up with mucky feet that will now be heavier and make your walk more uncomfortable, or instead step around that dreaded puddle and keep your feet light and dry as you happily continue moving forward.

The beautiful thing about seeing new light in all of these mundane and dreaded tasks is that your life takes on a whole new meaning, because as you find joy in all you do, you see how truly blessed you are, and gratefulness is the foundation to a life fulfilled with all of the good that God blesses you with.

love needs to flow

"Dear children, let us not love with words or speech,
but with actions and in truth."

1 John 3:18 NIV

Learning to Love

God tells us to love one another and this can be the most challenging commandment to obey, for people are human, and we hurt, judge, and disrespect each other whether intentional or not. So how do we love those whom we find it impossible to even like at best?

Well, love goes well beyond the feelings we have for each other, because loves true definition is based on how we treat one another. God tells us to be kind, patient, forgiving, respectful, and supportive of one another, and all of these things are a call to action, that go well beyond only a "feeling." Love is about placing our personal feelings aside and doing what is best for one another.

We love when we choose to be the bigger person by upholding these morals and values that God gives to us, no matter what our feelings are telling us. Emotions have many wonderful purposes, but in love, they are not our first priority. We love one another by honoring God's definition, and that only happens when we understand that love is an action.

God tells us to love our enemies, by turning the other cheek, giving them the coat off our back, and praying for them. He tells us to not seek revenge or dole out our own justice when we are hurt or offended, for He takes care of these things in His own loving righteous ways.

We turn the other cheek by not fighting back, we help those in need no matter what we feel or think about them. When we are judged, hurt, or disrespected, we pray to God to change the hearts of those that are bringing pain into our lives, and ask God for His power of forgiveness to let go of our bitterness towards them.

Many times love calls us to do nothing at all, as we exercise our self-control and let God take care of the things we cannot. The times we walk away from destructive situations instead of making them worse, the times we don't snap back at someone who is trying to put us down, or the times we just keep ourselves from doing what we know in our hearts is wrong: are also ways we act in love.

Love is all about righteous actions, when we choose to treat others with the same compassion, grace, and respect that God gives to us. It's not about whether someone deserves any of these things or not, for this is not up to us. True love is a conscious effort to follow God's will in all things, especially when it applies to our actions towards others.

Love isn't easy, especially when we are being mistreated by others, but when we love in the ways that God calls us to, we allow Him to work through us and bring more of Him into the world. Love nurtures love, and the more we give it away, the more it will come back to us, for God always blesses a heart that acts out of love.

right in front of you

"And my God will meet all your needs
according to the riches of his glory in Christ Jesus."

Philippians 4:19 NIV

Missing All You Have by Always Wanting More

Do you ever find yourself looking at life, thinking you just don't have enough and always wanting more? Not enough money, friends, time, or things to do: not enough "anything" to satisfy you?

Maybe you glance into the lives of others, wishing you had what they do; everyone else seems to have so much more than you, why don't you have that much "more" too?

Or how about that list you've created of all you want to achieve and acquire, that notebook living inside of your head with so many things you long to check off, to only make room to keep adding more things to "want."

The thing about always wanting more is that no matter how much "more" we get, we will never be truly satisfied, for the desire for more becomes our greatest craving of all. We want for things we do not have, we want for things we think we need to make us happier, and sometimes we want more of what we already have, just to have something more to want for!

There is nothing wrong to hope and long for more in our lives, but the problem arises when we get so consumed in that which we don't yet have, that it causes us to ignore all that God has already given to us. We take what we have for granted, become selfish in our desires, and when we don't get what we want, we end up with regrets that leave us feeling our lives will never be completely fulfilled. We can't see all that we truly have to be grateful for, when all of our "wants" keep telling us that we don't have enough.

The greatest "aha" moment I had in this reality was when I was so focused on wanting to have another child after going through two miscarriages. One child wasn't "enough;" I desperately needed to have at least one more to complete our "perfect" family.

I went through many tests and exploratory surgery, seeking answers to why I was losing these babies, only to find out that there was no clear cut medical reason as to why this was happening. As I got up to leave, my Doctor gently said to me, "You have a beautiful family, go and enjoy the life that you have with them." This simple sentence spoke a profound truth to me that day, a truth that changed my heart, my perspective, and turned my life around forever.

I realized that while I had been spending all of my time and energy focusing on the child I so desperately longed for, my eyes had become blinded to the blessing of the precious family that God had given me. I was missing the joy in all that I already had to be grateful for, by consuming myself with the more I believed I needed to be truly happy.

We will never be satisfied with what we have, if all we do is constantly look for more and wish for what we do not have. But, when we take a good look at all we have to be grateful for, all that God gives, provides, and blesses us with, we'll be able to find that joyful place of satisfaction in our hearts, as our need for more is replaced with a heart of gratitude, and a grateful heart always brings more than enough.

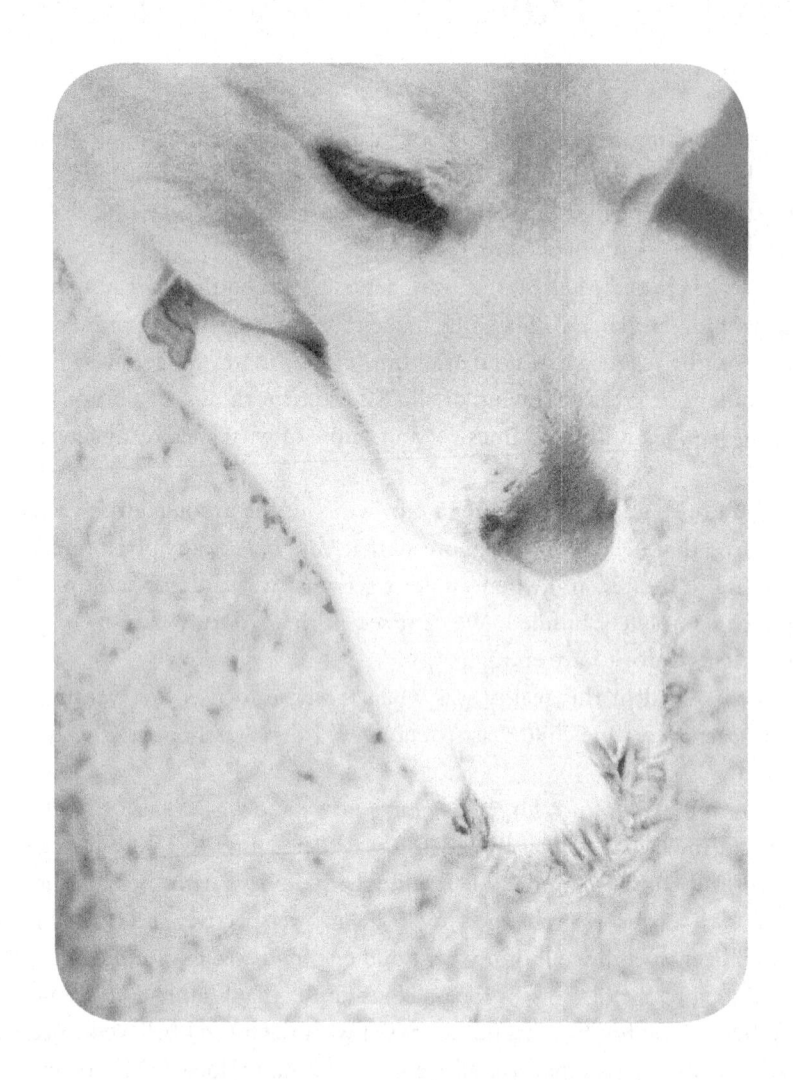

we all need to know that we matter

"Do nothing out of selfish ambition or vain conceit. Rather, in humility value others above yourselves, not looking to your own interests but each of you to the interests of others."

Philippians 2:3-4 NIV

Life Isn't a Competition

We live in such a competitive world that tells us the only way to succeed and be happy is to strive to be better than everyone else, no matter what the cost.

Competition can be beneficial in some areas of life, such as sports, contests, and fun group activities, when the purpose in doing so is meant to teach teamwork, support, and how to be humble and gracious with one another. But when we compete with others for the sole intention of proving that we are somehow better, stronger, or smarter than someone else, to feel like we are superior, we turn life's journey into a competitive game of ego, and someone will always be hurt.

We are all different, yet in many ways we are the same, for our strengths and weaknesses put us on the same playing field, as we pursue the purpose of our journey. No man stands alone in their successes, for we all receive some kind of assistance and support from God and through others; therefore, to boast that we did anything completely on our own is selfish, prideful and ungrateful.

God didn't place us here to "outdo" one another; He put us here to do life together, so that no one ever feels like a loser.

We all want many of the same things in life, and there's plenty to go around for each of us. Some of us will reach the finish line faster than others, while others will take a little longer, because the race is personal to each individual. Our goal to achieve more and be more in life, and to pursue all that God offers to each of us, can be a positive experience for everyone, as long as we do so with kindness, respect, and concern for one another. But when it becomes "all about us;" no one really wins anything at all.

As we attain all of our own personal objectives, God gives us wisdom, direction, and life lessons that are meant to share with the next person we meet on our path, to help them reach their own dreams and desires as well.

God blesses us through one another, and as we are blessed, we are called to bless others, by helping them with their own game plan, so everyone ends up winning in their own life journey.

When we realize that we are a wonderful team that God put together, instead of looking at life as a competition against each other, we can all become winners alongside one another.

walk on through

"Even so, when you see all these things,
you know that it is near, right at the door."

Matthew 24:33 NIV

Open the Door

Life is a hallway with many doors, and our choice is whether we open these doors and walk through the entrance, or whether we pass them by.

Doors are the beginnings to all of life's opportunities, blessings, and callings that God has prepared for each of us, and as we walk through them we find and fulfill our life purpose.

God places doors all along our life's path for all we need and so much more: entryways that lead us to healing, restoration, relationship, dreams, and direction.

Sometimes we see these doors clear as day, but other times they are harder to recognize when our doubts, worries, and desires of the flesh cast shadows upon the doorways that God has placed in front of us. We can miss many of God's invitations when we are too focused on only ourselves and our own expectations.

God holds the key to unlock every door we encounter. He waits patiently for us to arrive at each entrance, gently places that key in the palm of our hand, and steps over the threshold with us as we walk into that which awaits us beyond the door's entrance.

God's doors appear in many different ways throughout our lives. It may be a thought or feeling of intuition that comes through prayer or appears out of nowhere. Many times, it's a strong urging in your heart that lingers and never completely leaves you, no matter how hard you try to dismiss it. Sometimes it appears through the needs of others, or an unexpected situation He places you in.

His doors open "life" to us, and the doors we miss can leave us feeling sad and regretful when we eventually see why that door was so important and how we now wish we would have opened it. We miss the possibilities for forgiveness and restoration to only end up with damaged and lost relationships. That chance you didn't take because it was scary or uncomfortable, may have been the opportunity to begin the dream you've been longing for. Or maybe, the friend you've been meaning to call, but kept putting off, is suddenly gone and no longer there to reach out to at all.

But God is a God of second chances and will continue to build new doors for us to walk through, to replace the doors we ignored and passed by. He uses what we left behind in the hallway to nurture, strengthen, and teach us, so we will be able to see that next door of opportunity clearer than ever.

So, when you miss one door, don't quit or give up, keep walking and looking for that next door around the corner by opening your eyes wider to see His light shining upon the next door of opportunity He has waiting for you.

see "me" please

"Therefore, as God's chosen people, holy and dearly loved, clothe yourselves with compassion, kindness, humility, gentleness and patience."

Colossians 3:12 NIV

Seeing Life Through Other's Eyes

Life is so fast-paced and stressful these days, and we can become so focused on the things we're going through, that we forget that everyone else is going through their own "something" as well. Every person out there is dealing with more than we know, while they are living their own story with chapters not visible to us.

What we see on the surface is not their full story; it's only the current page they are on in their own life journey. We have no idea what the previous chapters in their life look like: the life events that led them to where they are today, nor the emotional scars they may be carrying deep within their hearts.

Someone may be doing their best in the place they are at, but we see their efforts as far from ideal because all we are focused on is what we need and what we believe is best for us.

When we neglect to expand our center of attention to see into the lives of others, we become self-centered, judgmental, and our hearts begin to turn hard toward one another. Many times, we set standards for others and expect them to handle life's situations in the same way that we do. We believe that their actions, reactions, and feelings should be in the same line of focus as ours, and when they aren't, we dismiss them.

We all deal with life differently, and our lives are not always on the same page, so in order to nurture compassion and understanding amongst one another, we need to look through the lenses of what others are seeing and going through.

I went through a few very rough years while I was separated from my husband: my Dad was sick and eventually died, and then my Mom had a stroke, bringing a total upheaval to every part of my life.

There were times I was judged by others for not doing enough, not doing it their way, and was also labeled as an overemotional person and told to get on with my life. They didn't see all that I was going through, nor did they care, because my best didn't meet their needs and expectations, and there was no grace or compassion offered beyond their own limited vision. I was a bother to them, and they couldn't "deal" with me, and so they walked away.

When people don't seem as they should be to us, we need to step back and ask ourselves why, taking into consideration that they are dealing with more than the situation at hand. They are troubled and hurting and doing their best, and it's up to us to be there for them.

God gives us peripheral vision to see well beyond what only lies directly in front of us in our own lives and a heart with the capacity to hold enough understanding and grace to offer to one another.

As we open our eyes to see into the lives of others, our vision becomes unlimited, and we are able to see others in much the same way that God sees each of us, so that we can treat each person with the same love and respect that we all need and deserve.

church—more than a building

"...so in Christ we, though many, form one body,
and each member belongs to all the others."

Romans 12:5 NIV

Church Hurt

The true meaning of church is when two or more gather together in Jesus name to worship God. Church is not about a fancy building or man-made rules to follow; church is relationship with God at its center. And because of its human relational side, church can cause pain and hurt in our lives, because people are fallible, and church is people.

Some churches follow the rules of religions that were formed thousands of years ago, while others that are so called "nondenominational" set up rules of their own. Yes, rules are necessary to keep order and focus, but in no way should they overshadow a church's true purpose.

But many times, church ends up being more about the rules it is trying to uphold, the mission it is pursuing, and the pride, status, and personal objectives of the people leading the church than about God. We can get caught up in so much "church" that we sometimes lose sight of its true definition. Leaders and those assigned to special duties sometimes allow their positions to go to their heads, thinking that they are somehow "better" than those whom they have been called to guide and support, and then church loses its focus, and this is when church can hurt people.

Churches are one of the most vulnerable places that become susceptible to cliques, gossip, and judgement, because church has a very personal meaning and purpose for each of us. When emotions and self-centered biases take over, harmful mistakes are made and people suffer.

For these very reasons, I went through tremendous hurt caused by a church I trusted and invested my heart in. The church became so much about their inner circle, that instead of being open and welcoming, they built walls of separation and made a lot of selfish choices that caused great harm to others.

Church is a place of trust, to feel safe, cared for, and accepted for who we are and can only maintain its integrity and serve God's purpose when we respect and acknowledge the value of each person's God given purpose. Church is a place where we go to learn graciousness, forgiveness, and compassion toward one another, in the same way that God loves each of us equally, no matter how different we are.

We are all part of one body, the body of Christ, here to support one another and never to judge, cast out, or cause harm to anyone. The main focus of any church should be to love, honor, and serve God and each other.

Church shouldn't hurt, make you question your Faith, or cause you to feel like you are less "Holy" than others, church is a place to nurture and grow us along our spiritual journeys.

Never feel pressured to remain in a church that brings trouble to your heart or persuades you to question your morals and values. God doesn't care about what building you enter; He cares more about your heart and His personal relationship with you.

God walks us through it

"I have told you these things, so that in me you may have peace.
In this world you will have trouble. But take heart! I have overcome the world."

John 16:33 NIV

God Didn't Do It

We've all heard the saying that God doesn't give us more than we can handle in life, but if we believe this to be true, then are we not saying that God is the one who intentionally brings pain and heartache to us?

Some people then go on to say that these are trials brought by God to test our faith, and personally, I so disagree with this. The God I believe in is all loving and wants only the best for us and would never do anything to cause harm or make our lives more difficult for any reason or purpose.

The problems, struggles, and heartaches we encounter here on this earth are not handed to us by God; they are a consequence of the imperfect world we live in. God never said life would be easy, and Jesus told us we would face trials and tribulations along our journeys here, and to believe that all the troubles we encounter are sent by God will only fill our hearts with fear, instead of Faith and trust in Him.

God doesn't want us to be afraid of Him; He wants us to trust Him with confidence, hope, and love in our hearts. The world isn't always kind, loyal, and honorable to us, but we do have a God who is continually faithful and committed to our lives.

The person dying of an incurable disease, the family that loses their home to a fire, or the wife who is being abused by her husband are not circumstances that were planned by God for any one of these people to "handle."

Whenever we are faced with more than we can handle on our own, God is the one who steps in and handles these things "for" us. He gives us His strength, comfort, and grace to get through all the tragedies and hardships that life brings our way. He hurts with us, He cries with us and walks right beside us when life brings us more than we can handle. His greatest desire is to take our suffering upon His shoulders and handle the pain that we cannot.

Life will always have moments of pain and suffering that won't make sense and may greatly test our Faith at times, but we must always remember that these things are not from God. When we are down on our knees and can no longer stand, because the weight of life's troubles are too heavy for us to carry, God is standing within us to keep us from bending too far and breaking.

His unwavering promise to never leave or forsake us is how God handles life "for" us, when we can't handle it all by ourselves.

write your best story

"But store up for yourselves treasures in heaven, where moths and vermin do not destroy, and where thieves do not break in and steal. For where your treasure is, there your heart will be also."

Matthew 6:20-21 NIV

What Legacy are You Creating?

I sometimes wonder what others will remember me for once I am no longer here; what will they say at my eulogy. Will my life be remembered for the kind of cars I drove, titles I held, money I left behind in my bank account, and all of the "stuff" I acquired?

Or will I be remembered for the smiles, laughter, inspiration, and memorable moments that I brought to the lives of others?

Will my life speak only to worldly success, or more to a giving, loving, and compassionate heart that touched the life of another person somehow, somewhere along my journey here?

Each day we have a choice to create our own legacy, by the choices we make in our priorities and the actions that speak to our characters and the person we truly are.

God gives us life, with free will to choose what we will do with this gift, giving us the wonderful opportunity to make our lives count for something greater, and to leave a lasting impression on others that will live on in them when we're no longer here.

When I look back at my parent's life, I see the inheritance they left me with, beyond the material things I acquired after their deaths. Their lives left me with priceless values and lessons that continue to play a huge part in my own life, precious gifts that I can now pass on to my daughter.

My Mom taught me to keep on keeping on no matter how hard life gets, and my Dad left with me a spirit to never stop learning and growing and to always trust God first in all things.

These are the legacies they built their lives upon and make my own choice very clear to me now. It's not about all I achieve and accumulate, the most important thing is the example I set by how I choose to live life and treat others.

The "things" I leave behind will be long gone and forgotten someday, but what will remain and live on is all that I did from a loving, faithful and compassionate heart that touched the lives of those who God placed along my path while I was here.

All we do that comes from our hearts will touch more lives than we can ever imagine and live on for many years after we're gone, more than any number of "things" we accumulate during our time here on earth.

Think about what legacy you want to leave and begin creating your beautiful heritage today.

family

"...so in Christ we, though many, form one body,
and each member belongs to all the others."

Romans 12:5 NIV

The True Meaning of "Family"

When you hear the word "family" who are the first people that enter your mind? I bet more than likely you think of your parents, children, siblings, etc.; anyone closely connected to you who comes from the same lineage and bloodline that you do.

Yet when you look back in time to the place of God's original creation of humanity; when Adam and Eve were the first humans set on God's path to begin procreation, you can see that we all originated from this beautiful beginning.

God created family when He breathed His life into these two human beings, and He continues to breath life into each new person who is born to keep His family growing. When you look at it this way, it's plain to see, that we are all His children...we are all family. But of course it's impossible to be intricately connected to millions of people, so we tend to look at family as those with whom we are closely bonded to; our traceable lineage.

Family, however, goes well beyond only these people, for family extends itself farther and wider as God connects us with so many others throughout the course of our lives. Family is relationship, front and center, and God doesn't limit us to only those we share the same genetics with. Sometimes the family we are given through traceable DNA, aren't always the ones we have the closest relationships with, for people are each unique and live their lives differently, and we don't always intimately connect with or even get along with those in our immediate family circle. God understands this and therefore He brings others into our lives, that become "true" family in its purest meaning.

Those who choose to be a part of our life; those who choose to love and accept us for who we are, and those people who walk life with us, for no other reason than they genuinely love and care about us are all family to us. The people that God sends to encourage, support and lift us up, whether we came from the same parents and their family extensions or not, are what defines family in its truest form. This is how God extends the love of family to each of us; a gift to be cherished over and over.

God is the Father to all of us, and will always continue to connect the hearts of those that need each other; creating His perfect definition of family for each and every one of us.

disquieted emotion

"Humble yourselves, therefore, under God's mighty hand,
that he may lift you up in due time."

1 Peter 5:6 NIV

Peace in the Unknown

One of our greatest human needs in life is certainty; the assurance that we can depend on that which we trust and believe to be concrete and stable. We believe that the more that we know, somehow prepares and protects us to make our lives safer, by leaving no room for unexpected surprises that can turn our lives upside down in a moments notice.

But reality shows us that there are many things in life we will never completely know, for life is full of so many unknowns: those gray areas in life that aren't that clear, test our beliefs, mess with our peace of mind, and awaken our fears anytime we become unsure of things. The times we spend waiting for answers we have no control over, the times other people's choices and decisions may disrupt our own lives, and all of the things we worry and think about that could possibly happen leave us in a vulnerable place of uncertainty.

I am an over-anxious thinker, and I like to try to figure out every possible scenario, so I can be prepared for any unknown thing that is heading my way. But, this kind of thinking only makes me more anxious and unsure of anything at all, because now I've created more unknowns to be concerned about than those I initially started with.

Our need for certainty can be somewhat a breach of trust in our relationship with God, because nothing in life is that simple. Our human desire to always want to know everything can relay the message that we are in control, while no longer placing our complete trust in the ONE who will always know more than we do. As we let go of our fear of uncertainty, we receive the peace "not of this world" that Jesus promised: a peace that can only be found in the Spirit within us.

God protects us, guides us, and pleasantly surprises us when we hand over our worry and fear and trust Him in every Unknown we encounter.

Don't be afraid of that which you do not know; instead, wait in the peace you received from Jesus and enjoy every moment of the life right in front of you, while entrusting the rest to Him.

new seeds to nurture new blessings

"...which is his body, the fullness of him who fills everything in every way."

Ephesians 1:23 NIV

God Fills in the Empty Spaces

I'm not one for New Year's Resolutions, 5-year goals, or anything like that. It's not that I don't believe in self ambitions and making plans; I just don't look too far ahead in anything. Life is fickle and more often than not, changes "my" plans, so I don't hold onto my own desires too tightly, and that way I'm never too disappointed when my plans don't work out the way I expected them to.

Instead, I leave my life open to every possibility, and the plans that God is preparing and will place along my path, which are always better than any goal I could set by myself.

So, at the end of every year, I look "back" and not forward, and am always amazed and humbled at all that God brought, changed, and led me toward. At the end of every year, I thank Him for everything; the trials, the challenges, and of course all of His blessings, that made me stronger, wiser, and brought me closer to Him.

These things that are now my past are not to be left behind and forgotten, for it is through all of these things blended together that will prepare me for the new year ahead and all of the possibilities waiting for me.

My only "resolution" for any new year is to become more of the person God created me to be. Yes, I have things I would like to achieve, but I am always willing to change my hopes, plans, and desires when God shows me something different. His plans are always greater than mine, and as long as I leave myself some leeway to go with His flow and not get stubbornly stuck in my own way and will, my life is fulfilled with more than anything I alone could ever imagine or dream of.

2017 was a challenging year for me, with the loss of my Mom, the damaged relationships with my siblings, the unexpected passings of some very dear friends, as well as the loss of my church and those I totally trusted.

But in all of this loss, God filled in the sad and empty places of my heart. He showed me truth to set me free from that which was harming me, he brought new relationships into my life to show me the true meaning of family, and connected me to the hearts of those He calls me to love and encourage, through the gift of writing that He has blessed me with. He opened new doors of wonderful opportunities, and most importantly, He walked with me through all of this and never stopped loving me, no matter how tough some of these roads were to travel.

God will never waste any experience I go through, for He always brings something more to replace anything that was lost and forgotten.

Always look back over each year of your life, no matter how difficult a season it was, and open your eyes and heart to see all of the good God brought to you and trust Him to continue to fill in every empty space within you that is waiting for more of His goodness.

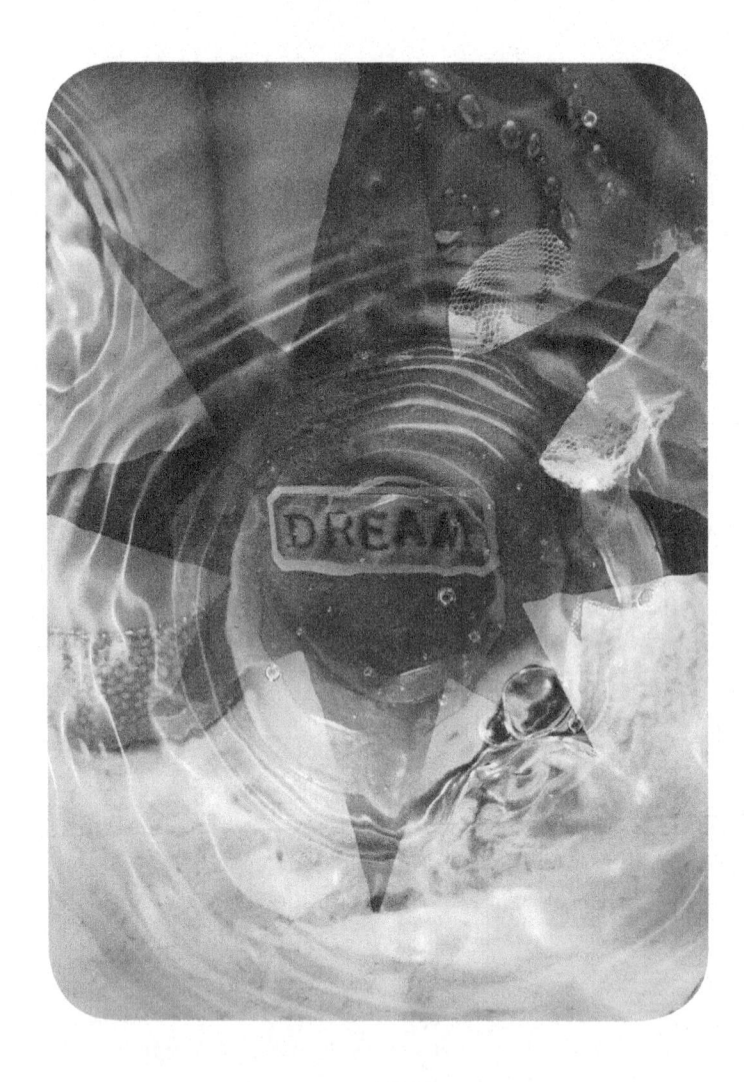

always and forever

"Take delight in the Lord, and he will give you the desires of your heart."

Psalm 37:4 NIV

A Dream's Destination Never Ends

I believe life is an unending dream journey. Dreams are our ambitions, hopes and all we aspire to, which come from the special and unique talents and gifts that God plants within each of us.

The seeds within to be watered and nurtured, to build our life's purpose and bring us joy, are where dreams are born and continue to grow when we allow them to.

Yet, many times when we begin our dream journey, we give it a final destination, that end that we believe will fulfill that dream and bring us all of the happiness that we so desire.

But just as life has many twists and turns, and reasons and seasons, so do dreams, and there's a beautiful explanation for that: Dreams aren't meant for only one destination, for dreams are not meant to ever end.

To put a specific final vision to any one dream, not only places limits on our dream endeavor, but can be quite bittersweet when we reach the end. But what if we looked at those dreams as a new and greater opportunity for the dream to grow into something even more amazing?

One of the biggest dreams I've ever had was to start my own business; let go of that corporate paycheck and be my own boss. I'm blessed with the gift of creativity and so I began this new journey. I began making unique and useful pieces of cork and clay art, along with a line of bracelets that were quite successful. I did art shows and sold my items on line and in a few local stores.

At first it was fun and exciting and I had great visions, but as time went on I was spending more money than I was making, and the time, work, and effort it took was draining me, as well as ruining the vision I had for the dream. After two and a half years full of numerous challenges, I let go of the dream, feeling more defeated than ever.

It wasn't until a few years later that I was able to see the true purpose of this dream and all of the wonderful blessings it left me with. The wonderful people that crossed my path, the lessons I learned from being a business owner, the things I accomplished beyond anything I ever thought possible, and the spirit to persevere were just some of the gifts that God brought to me while pursuing this one—but not only—dream on my journey.

And although this dream journey had reached its end, God placed a new dream in front of me; using my gift of writing to publish this book that you are now reading. And this won't be the last dream adventure I'll go on, for I fully know and believe that God has the next one waiting for me, and I can't wait to see what that will be.

Pursue every dream as you trust in the journey and not the final destination, for it is in the journey that you will find a life full of dreams that will lead you from one beautiful dream journey to the next...and the next.

Connect With Sue

Join Sue's "A Little Somethin' Somethings" Facebook community at

https://www.facebook.com/Alittlesomethinsomethings

Blessings!

Made in the USA
Monee, IL
04 December 2019